Feng Shui For Writers

M.C. SIMON

HOW TO MASTER YOUR LIFE

Series

MW00880652

Feng Shui For Writers

Copyright © 2015 M.C. Simon

All rights reserved.

Published by IML Publishing
www. imlpublishing.us   info@imlpublishing.us

Purchaser is the sole authorized user of this information. No part of this publication may be reproduced, distributed or transmitted for resale or use by any party, in any form or by any means, including photocopying, recording, or other electronic or mechanical methods, without the prior written permission of the author/publisher, except in the case of brief quotations and certain other noncommercial uses permitted by copyright law.

ISBN: 151425994X

ISBN-13: 978-1514259948

Editor: Bogdan Stancu
Proofreading: Bogdan Stancu
Layout: Internet Marketing Light
Cover design & photos: Internet Marketing Light
www.InternetMarketingLight.com

FIRST EDITION: JUNE 2015
First Printing

DISCLAIMER

This book is designed to provide condensed information. The author does not intend to present all the information that is available, but instead to complement, amplify and supplement other existing texts. You are urged to read all the available material, learn as much as possible and tailor the information to your individual needs. Every effort has been made to prepare this book as complete and as accurate as possible. However, there may be mistakes, both typographical and in content. Therefore, this text should be used only as a general guide and not as the ultimate source of information. The author and publisher are not offering the book as legal, accounting, medical, educational or other professional services advice. While best efforts have been used in preparing this book, the author and publisher disclaim all such representations and warranties, including for example warranties of merchantability and educational or medical advice for a particular purpose. In addition, the author and publisher do not represent or warrant that the information accessible via this book is accurate, complete or current. Neither the author nor the publisher shall be held liable or responsible to any person or entity with respect to any loss or incidental or consequential damages caused, or alleged to have been caused, directly or indirectly, by the information contained herein. No warranty may be created or extended. Before you begin any change in your lifestyle in any way, you will consult a licensed professional to ensure that you are doing what is best for your situation. You should seek the services of a competent professional before beginning any improvement program. As such, use of this book implies your acceptance of this disclaimer.

TABLE OF CONTENTS

ACKNOWLEDGMENTS

To all the writers and bloggers whom I've met on the Path,
Thank you all for inspiring me each moment.

Special thanks to my editor who had the infinite patience with so many written phases before deciding on the final form of the book.

Last but not least, many thanks to my wonderful friends who accepted to play the role of beta-readers (B.J. Tiernan, J.R. Richards, Adriana Yamane and Arthur Karapetyan), and helped me so much with their advice and encouragement.

PREFACE
THE REASON FOR WRITING THIS BOOK

I am a human being passionate about knowledge; even if it is earthen tridimensional or multidimensional knowledge.

One of my domains of interest is working with energies. And for sure one of my all-time favorites is the old art of Feng Shui.

There are many good books on this subject, and maybe you are wondering why publish another one now. The answer is simple and complicated also; because it involves a personal story.

I will not describe the story now, but I will point out the main theme of it. Due to a decision that I recently made to change my career and to admit that I am a writer, I really studied hard to make my wish come truth. Being passionate about Feng Shui also, I realized that even if there are plenty of good books on working with energies in this way, I couldn't find any book specialized for writers.

For this reason, I decided to write one. And the result of this process is based on years of research, studies and experiments. Falling in love with my new "job" as a writer and understanding very well the special needs of anyone who loves to write, I really believe that you can make your life easier if you have the general knowledge on how to attract the positive energies around you.

I will not deny the need for contacting a specialist in certain cases. There are so-called impossible situations where you really encounter lots of obstacle in attracting what you need. In all the other cases that do not need special assistance, I consider that it is enough for you to live by applying the general rules of this ancient science and art, thereby positively influencing your life.

The main idea which I want to share with you is that in life we can and need to be self-appointed "experts" in as many domains as possible, to always handle and to understand why what is happening is happening; and this is because only through understanding and feeling, can we transform any event into something useful for our advancement.

No… don't finish your thought… You can be good in many domains of knowledge if your heart is commending you to do so. The old belief that you can be an expert only in one domain can still be valuable if we are talking about the tridimensional world. It's been a long time since humanity stepped into other perceptions, far beyond the material world we used to live in.

INTRODUCTORY WORD

Advice: DON'T read this book
if you coincidentally prefer to block your Muse.

"Being a writer myself, I recently started to work on my first novel. This book is intended to be a mix of romances, fantasy, paranormal, spiritual and probably some more genres. While preparing the plot for the book, I decided to include hidden meanings between the lines, so all type of readers would find more than just words and facts inside. The book will be written with a personal technique (yes, I am very creative). Depending on the level the reader has reached on the spiritual ladder, the written words will uplift and bring to surface knowledge already known; this knowledge was blocked or forgotten when the choice was made to come on this planet and into these human bodies.

To make the explanation short, while I was working on the novel, I realized that my surroundings didn't influence me as I wanted.

I suddenly noticed that the Chi flow around my desk and office was stagnant for what I needed to write. Instantly the cogwheels in my brain started working at a high-speed level, and a new creative idea was born... I have to Feng Shui my office, to let the Chi flow freely, to accurately boost my environment for this writing project. I did it... and for some time I wrote like never before; I almost couldn't be stopped by any external influences.

But... after a while I realized something; I couldn't keep this information only to myself. I had to share it with my fellow writers. Thus started the process I dubbed "the birth of my second first book". Yes, like this I referred to my project through which the book "Feng Shui for Writers" was born. I called it "the birth" because even the smallest ideas we have, cross through a birth process before manifesting into this world. I called it "my second first book" because it is my first published book, but the second one to be implemented and emerge from the embryo phase.

And this book was born **for YOU - the Writer!**"

(M.C. Simon - Feng Shui for Writers, Chapter 6.3 - The Creative Mind)

I had to copy this passage. I had to do it even if it was meant to be written in another chapter. It is the best explanation of why this book was born and what it's about.

In this book, I am not giving you advice about writing techniques.

Instead, I will share with you what I know about how to use the ancient technique of Feng Shui, to organize around you the energies in such a way to successfully influence your writing mood and skills; and most of all to build a deep relation with your personal Muse.

What I want you to understand from the beginning is that everything is inside you; you lack nothing. You only have to connect the dots.

My only intention in writing this book is to share with anyone interested, information about how you can play with these energies, without asking you to have deep knowledge of Feng Shui; without drawing complicated Feng Shui maps which will only succeed to make you dizzy and finally necessitate you to call a Feng Shui specialist to have them tell you exactly what you need to do.

No way! Not my style!

My only style was, is and will always be… Do It Yourself! You can do it!

I am not stating that I am a Feng Shui Master and I must mention that there are special cases in life when you really need one. What you read now comes from a writer who conducted her life according with the general rules of Feng Shui, among other rules related with what I am calling "playing with energies".

Saying that I want to make everyone understand how to apply the information included in this book, oblige me to start from a very beginner level; the basement level.

Don't worry… I will be very short about it. I'm sure that nearly everyone has already heard about this ancient art, but just in case there is one incarnated soul among us who still hadn't uncovered this information, let me sketch out the basics.

1
YOU DON'T LACK ANYTHING!

As I already said, I want you to understand from the beginning that everything is inside you; you lack nothing. You only have to connect the dots. If we agreed on this point, let's proceed!

What am I referring to? What do I mean by saying that you lack nothing?

And what about connecting the dots?

Let me explain these terms, so we can begin our talk from the same baseline.

I noticed during this lifetime that people don't know how to have a conversation; not because they don't know how to use words or merely not smart enough to express a phenomenal idea. I am pointing here only to the art of having a conversation with someone; and not an external monolog.

I am not stating that people don't want to hear what others are saying. But somehow, even if the intentions are good, still people can't touch the middle line when it is about conversation. The only reason I noticed is that prior to starting a dialog, people don't have the same definition equivalence. So even if they seem that they argue, in fact, people say the same things; only that they don't realize it.

Now... permit me to explain some terms (of course according to what I understand about using them; and this because I am the author, so I have the obligation of correctly conveying the meaning of my language); in this way we will assure ourselves that we both understand the same thing when a word is read.

I will try (and hope to succeed) to tell you more about:

What's a lack?

What do I mean by saying you don't lack anything?

What are the dots that must be connected?

How can we connect the dots?

How can we use the ancient art of Feng-Shui to connect all the dots needed?

Let's proceed!

1 - What's a lack?

What Merriam-Webster dictionary says about a *lack* is that it is something that you do not have, or something that you do not have enough of.

I very well agree with this statement if we are referring to material things. But my opinion is that internally we don't lack anything.

2 - What do I mean by saying you don't lack anything?

When we came into this world, and we chose these human bodies, we came equipped with all that we need to handle this life. For some reasons, during our lifetime, we forgot this and due to environmental influences, we start to believe that we are not able to do many things.

I include here the fact that we believe that we are not in charge of several situations and only if we meet certain expectations, can we solve many of the problems that we encounter on our path.

If we learned to listen to our hearts, we would find ways to access all of what we need.

3 - What are the dots that must be connected?

I call *dots* all the separate knowledge that we remember or we develop through our studies. I find it to be so funny this vicious circle in which we are moving in. Speaking about the dots... I see things belonging to this kind of circle.

We don't lack anything and to remember and understand this, we need to connect the dots that we possess so everything will become again as a whole. And when the dots are connected, we will feel that in fact we never lacked anything.

4 - How can we connect the dots?

How can we do this? Again here, we have a simple and complicated answer at the same time. It's simple because all of what we need, in fact, is the trust in ourselves and our capacities to access any information and to apply it to our lives. At the same time, the answer is complicated because our only problem is the lack of trust; the belief that there is no lack. This can be a subject for another book so I will not develop the theme here; just wanted to point it out.

5 - How can we use the ancient art of Feng Shui to connect all the needed dots?

To use the technique, we first need to know what it is about. In the following chapters, this subject will be developed in such a way that you will do it yourself. And you will see the difference soon.

After you find the necessary details, all you need to do is reach a clear intent. This is essential when you Feng Shui your home because you can never get what you are longing for if you don't know your destination.

To avoid slow, temporary or incomplete changes, before doing any adjustments to your writing environment, you have to follow some easy steps:

1 - First of all, you must open your heart and mind. You have to understand that everything is touched by energy; in fact, everything is energy itself. All that is energy is alive no matter if it belongs to the material world or the spiritual one. Finally, there is only one world, called the World of Infinity and only our belief that there exist multiple worlds makes us individually perceive the layers of the One. At the moment when we understand that in fact WE are divine creators and that everything is energy, we will start our conscious travel in this life. A travel which is supposed to be fun and to give us the happiness of being part of this whole process called experiencing life in a human body. So, open your mind and have fun.

2 - Clarify the intention for wanting to apply the Feng Shui techniques. Defining your purpose, motivation and intention, you will rapidly notice the results. Only by doing this will you start to make changes and apply this ancient art; only after first clarifying these aspects, will things begin to manifest almost instantly. Of course, you can choose first to apply the technique and only after much time start to understand fully what your intention is. But I am coming now to ask you, "Why should you choose to do this and prolong the period of manifestation"?

3 - When you start to make the changes, do them slowly; one by one to give you time to observe the effects of your actions. Keep alive your intention and continue to apply what you've learned.

2
WHO IS A WRITER?

Do you somehow think that a writer is someone who writes books; eventually best sellers?

Wrong! Let me explain who is a writer!

First, let us see what the definition says: a writer is a person who uses written words in various styles and techniques to express ideas. Generally speaking, the world accepts the statement that a writer produces various forms of literary art and creative writing. Their work can have multiple variants and depending on this, they are called: poets, novelists, satirists, lyricists, librettists, playwrights, speechwriters, screenwriters, biographers, critics, editors, encyclopedists, essayist, lexicographers, historians, researchers, scholars, translators, bloggers, diarists, journalists, columnists, memoirists, letter writers, ghostwriters, technical writers, scribes, report writers, writers of sacred texts.

- **Poets** are those creative writers who are using rhyme and rhythm to transform the language in tools to achieve emotional states.

- **Novelists** are creative writers who are using fiction to tell their stories that are called novels.

- **Satirists** are creative writers who are using sharpness to ridicule any shortcoming.

- **Lyricists** are performative writers who use verses that accompany a song.

- **Librettists** are those performative writers who create texts for musical works such as operas.

- **Playwrights** are also performative writers who usually write plays that are supposed to be performed by actors on a stage.

- **Speechwriters** are the performative writers who prepare persuasive and inspiring texts for a speech.

- **Screenwriters** are also performative writers, and they create screenplays, called scripts, for films and television programs.

- **Biographers** are interpretative writers who write about another person's life.

- **Critics** are interpretative and academic writers who assess if a work succeeded in its purpose. They can understand and incorporate the theory behind the work they are evaluating.

- **Editors** are interpretative writers who prepare written materials for publication.

- **Encyclopedists** are academic writers who compile and write a work that contains information on all branches of knowledge often arranged alphabetically by subject.

- **Essayists** are interpretative writers who create original pieces of writing which makes a case in support of an opinion.

- **Lexicographers** are academically writers who create dictionaries.

- **Historians** are also academically writers who write and study about the past.

- **Researchers** are scholar writers who write about their discoveries that can have a great impact on society.

- **Translators** are interpretative writers who have a big cultural influence transforming the words from a language to another.

- **Bloggers** are classified as reportage writers who write online opinions that need no authorization to be published.

- **Diarists** are also reportage writers who record and express in written words their thoughts and experiences.

- **Journalists** are those reportage writers who write reports on current events after investigating them.

- **Columnists** are reportage writers who regularly write for newspapers and periodicals.

- **Memoirists** also considered reportage writers who produce selective memoirs of their own lives.

- **Letter writers** are utilitarian writers who know to use words to transmit messages between individuals.

- **Ghostwriters** are utilitarian writers who write on behalf of another person who will take all the credit for that writing.

- **Technical writers** are also utilitarian writers who prepare manuals and guides.

- **Scribes** are utilitarian writers who write ideas on behalf of another person most of the time based on oral instruction.

- **Report writers** are those utilitarian writers who gather and document information to present to someone who needs to base a decision.

- **Writers of sacred texts** are those writers who write spiritual and religious texts or scriptures.

From the above classification, we somehow conclude that a writer is a person who makes a living from this process. This is true, but we have to add here that someone can be a writer even if their main job is something other than officially a writer. As the definition states, a writer is anyone who uses written words to express ideas. Extending this statement we can say that even someone who is writing a letter is also called a writer. You can permanently be a writer, or you can temporarily be one. Permanently or not, the moments when you want to start writing you need to have a special mood and be in touch with what is called "your Muse." Sometimes this Muse can't be sensed around the writer, so no inspiration will seem to show up on paper. But if we have some elementary knowledge of energies and how to work with them, we can attract all the inspiration that we need for our work to be done.

Nowadays all that a writer needs is a computer and some discipline to write while spending most of the time giving to the world their emotions and intellect.

It is necessary for the writer to have a space where they can give life to their future creation. Even if this writing place is a home or office space, a proper location is a must.

3
WHAT IS FENG SHUI?

3.1 - THE PRINCIPLES OF FENG SHUI

To understand the principles of Feng Shui, we must first understand what Feng Shui is.

In many cases, to understand what something is, it is easier for us to start grasping what that thing isn't. When I talk about Feng Shui, somehow I find it inappropriate to start with this; for the only reason that Feng Shui can be all things. It is a concept, a technique, an ancient art that finally stands behind anything; that is because all is energy and Feng Shui masters energies.

I will not mention the history of it here because we have a separate section for this aspect.

Feng Shui is one of the Five Arts (Chinese Astrology Bazi or Four Pillars of Destiny, Feng Shui, Divination, Chinese medicine and Mian Xiang - Face reading) of Chinese metaphysics, classified as physiognomy of the living environment (*physys* meaning nature and *gnomon* meaning judge or interpreter).

It approaches the architecture of the so-called Chi, the invisible force that populates the universe, earth and man altogether. Feng Shui is, in fact, an art of improving the quality of life through analysis of the person's environment.

In our days, most of the people consider that Feng Shui is a fashion and a decorating art. In truth, it is not and will never be related to fashion; more than this, Feng Shui is a science, one of the most ancient sciences we know. It is about Chi in the living environment and it explains how to use this Chi to help with specific goals. Also, Feng Shui is a form of forecasting. Many practitioners today neglect this characteristic. However, if we know the types of Chi that will affect an environment in a specific year or month of the year, we can Feng Shui the place to be prepared and overcome any situation.

Together with Destiny and Human factors, Chi is one of the three cosmic components which influence our lives. For this reason, the ancient art of Feng Shui is not a miracle cure but a technique of harnessing the Chi. Feng Shui must be approached with an open mind and the goal for its use should never be forgotten.

Using this art, we will transform our environment into a very comfortable and beautiful place. This will also affect our physical and mental health, as well as our success and relationships.

Feng Shui examines how the flow of energy is influenced by the placement of objects around us. These objects affect our personal energy flow, therefore also the way in which we are thinking and acting. As we already know, the way we think and act influences everything in our lives. So we find ourselves in a vicious circle; for this reason we need to adapt our surrounding to have a good start - a beneficial flow of energy.

What we need to understand is that Feng Shui is not a quick method for becoming rich, it is not another design and fashion art, it is not a method that can be used only by rich people but can and should be used by any person no matter of his financial status or social position.

Explained and being seen only at its surface, Feng Shui is the method of interaction between man and his environment. But digging some more, this technique is, in fact, a method that people can use to influence the environment to achieve a specific goal in their life. Through Feng Shui, understanding and working with the flow of energy, man can achieve harmony in life.

When we decide to Feng Shui a space in which we live, we decide, in fact, to bring comfort and balance in our life; and we do this on every level that we perceive or not.

If we look into the etymology of this name, we notice that it is a term composed of two Chinese words: Feng and Shui that mean wind and water.

These two natural elements flow and circulate anywhere on Earth. Man can live a long time without other natural elements, but these two are the basic for his survival. Without air (breath) we would leave these bodies almost instantly. Without water, which is the liquid of life, we would survive only a few days.

The combination of these two natural elements, determines everything during our lives, from lifestyle to health and mood. If the individual is influenced, then the society will also be influenced. If the individual is healthy in all aspects than the human society will also be healthy.

Feng Shui has roots in the holistic perception of the world. According to this technique, all things are equally alive and have an energetic meaning and value; through all things the same energy flows.

Feng Shui divides the vast field of energy that circulates in this universe in smaller units like humans, plants, properties, homes, etc. Of course, we can't control the energy that flows in the entire universe but we can influence the flow in these smaller units, arranging the environment in a proper way.

The Chi flows through our bodies and also through our living spaces. If this energy is stagnant (the case of an overloaded closet), it moves too quickly (like long dark halls) or is obstructed (walls or trees placed in wrong places), the Chi becomes unbalanced and this can lead to illness, domestic problems, financial issues and even loss of business.

Through applying the technique of Feng Shui, all these problems can be repaired, canceled out, and good health, harmony, and prosperity will return.

The practitioners of Feng Shui, on the one hand, must know very well the influences of each natural element over the flowing Chi and on the other hand they must know how to listen to their intuition. I already stated at the beginning of this book that we don't lack anything and inside us we have all the knowledge of the universe. We must only bring peace inside of us and listen to our hearts. And these hearts (which, of course, are not the physical hearts) will access for us and bring to surface all that we need to know. Being human, it is not so easy for us to totally listen to our intuition, but with proper study, we can help ourselves in accessing it.

Keep in mind to always use the hidden wisdom which will come to the surface for our highest good as we learn to trust more in ourselves. Do this in your intention and observe the difference in time. We are more powerful than we think we are.

Feng Shui techniques increases positive energy around us; doing this, our intention is more focused on our goals, and through the subliminal messages that are suddenly perceived by us, the space around us becomes sacred and more than this, we can feel this sacredness.

Life is based on decisions; one decision that we must make in life is to choose what kind of path we want to have; a light path filled with satisfaction and understanding of the reasons for which all that is happening has to happen, or a cluttered path filled with worries, illness, and obstacles. I am not preaching now saying that if we use Feng Shui we will live our daily life in bliss only… I already said that the flow of Chi is the third component of the cosmic influences that paves our lives. What I intended to state, is the fact that using it, we will be able to influence, to correct and to heal the life aspects that depend on this Chi.

A long time ago, the Chinese studied the differences and the connections between people who were born rich and those born poor. They noticed that some of those who were not born with a so-called silver spoon in their mouth succeeded to change somehow and control the path that they were meant to have in life. These changes and controls were not about good luck... but were about decisions they have taken.

So... Silence your mind! Control your intention! Decide well and go for life!

3.2 - A LITTLE HISTORY

There are several points of view regarding Feng Shui's history. It seems that both China and India claim the origin of this ancient art.

About 5,500 years ago in India, the mystics practiced a technique called "Vastu Shastra" which was a system that explained how to design and construct localities and buildings based on the effects of the five elements - earth, water, fire, air and space. In old scripts, it is mentioned that about 3,000 years ago, the Indian monks who practiced this technique crossed the Tibet area and settled themselves in China were they taught the Vastu principle.

Whether this is a correct variant or not, it was obviously 3000 - 4000 years ago that the Chinese people used a method of burial that evolved over time and which had the same principle as what later become known as Feng Shui.

Between 1030-722 B.C, during the Chou dynasty, the Chinese wrote "The Book of Ritual" that described the best methods to place and build a city; and where its gates would be placed compared with the four compass points.

Around the year 1970-1980, the Feng Shui technique started to be used in United States also and after this it was developed in Europe and Australia.

The books on Feng Shui sometimes seem to contradict each other, and the reason is the fact that over the span of so many years, this ancient technique has developed in several different directions, which formed various schools. The main principles are similar and, even though, the details can differ, it only means that to achieve the desired result, you can use more than one way.

For thousands of years, the art of Feng Shui was perceived as the "emperor's magic". The technique was kept secret by the priests who closely guarded it. Only recently, the boundaries between Eastern and Western civilizations were shattered, and the whole world could now learn about it.

As the time passed by, there were various schools, and I will mention the most known bellow:

The Kanyu school - is considered the precursor of all Feng Shui Schools and was using time and space in a prognosticary system that was choosing the fortunate locations. In principle it relied strictly on astrology and numerology; while Feng Shui is local, the Kanyu is universal.

The Form school (also called Xingfa) - is the oldest form of documented Feng Shui. It was concerned with the orientation of tombs and later on with the buildings used for living. The chi flow, transformational elements and the terms like yin and yang were of this school's interest. It used terrestrial things that serve to block the wind (that catch Chi and exude it) and channel the waters (which catch Chi and retain it). This school focuses on land formations and the house's surrounding environment, stating that the exterior elements have the greatest impact on the building.

The Compass school (also called Lifa or Cosmological school) - is based on numerical calculations determined using a western compass or a Chinese luo pan. Analyses are based on what is called Bagua. Sometimes they were taking into account the birthdays of the involved persons, so the relation between that person and the environment would be touched at a deeper level.

The Modern School (also called Three Gates) - is a modern western school that is targeting different aspects of life and it aligns the Bagua with the front door.

3.3 - WHAT IS CHI?

At the beginning of this Chapter, we already mentioned the term Chi; for understanding what Feng Shui is, we have to use it. I tried to talk about Chi only on the surface, intending to dig further in this subchapter. I wanted to have a Title especially about Chi because I don't want this information to be lost between the words and lines; and I want you to always find, easy details about this important notion.

Chi... is a concept... an element that lays at the heart of Feng Shui. Chi is the energy that exists in all things. It circulates in our bodies, in our houses, in our gardens, in our cities. Chi is the energy found in rivers, in wind, in mountains, in deserts. Chi is everywhere, the Yin (the female, yielding energy) and the Yang (the male, penetrating force) winds through everything around us.

When this energy is strong, it creates mountains, rivers, and prosperous environments. When Chi is weak, valleys and deserts are created. Feng Shui locates the Chi and attracts it to where we want and need it to be.

When Chi meets the Feng (wind) is scattered but when it encounters Shui (water) it is retained. The technique described here is about preventing the Chi dispersal and assuring its retention.

To give a proper definition to this term, Chi, the English language doesn't seem to define it enough. We are calling it energy and doing this, some of its characteristics are touched but the metaphysical aspects do not even reach the surface.

Before our Era, Chi was defined as a meteorological category composed of six stages of warmth, cold, rain, wind, darkness, and light.

Later it was said that Chi flows where the earth changes shape. Terrestrial traits serve to block the wind (which captures Chi and scatters it) and channel the waters (that collect Chi and store it).

Generally speaking, the Chinese believe that Chi is the energy that governs the life force in all living beings and matter. Chi literally means air or breath, but we should not think of Chi in this sense; it will seriously limit our understanding.

A great scientist named Zhang Dai, who lived during the Song Dynasty, said: "The Chi has both positive and negative qualities. When Chi spreads out, it permeates all things; it becomes nebulous. When it settles into form, it becomes matter. When it disintegrates, it returns to its original state."

The Chinese divide Chi in two opposite forces: yin (female) and yang (male). To have a healthy body and life, Chi must be balanced. For this, the yin and yang must be in a total equilibrium. If, in our bodies an imbalance is caused, the health imbalance will also follow.

The imbalance inside our bodies is caused by the imbalance of our environment. For this reason, we must balance the yin and yang of all that is around us.

Chi can be positive or negative. Positive Chi is known as Sheng Chi also called Living Chi while Negative Chi is called Shar Chi; translated Killing Chi. In the technique of Feng Shui, Sheng Chi improves wealth, heath, relationships, etc. while Shar Chi causes accidents, illness, etc.

3.4 - THE FIVE ELEMENTS

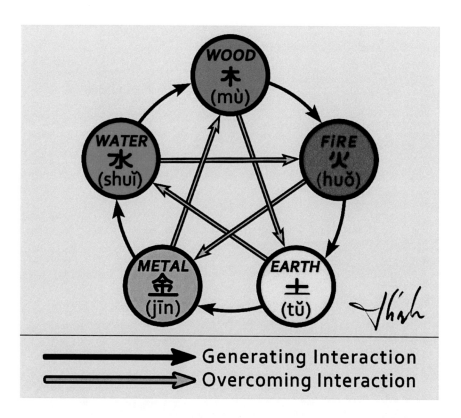

The palpable aspects of Feng Shui are given to us by the Five elements (each of them is unique and has specific colors and shapes):

Water:

- A catalyst element

- The specific colors are: blue, dark blue, and black

- The characteristic shape is wavy
- The particular material is glass
- The appropriate objects: aquarium, water features, wavy patterns, mirrors, water scenes

Fire:

- A catalyst element
- The specific colors are: red and orange
- The characteristic shape is triangle
- The particular material is electricity
- The appropriate objects: computer, candles, lamps, fireplace, pyramids, obelisks, spires, animal prints

Wood:

- A content element
- The specific colors are: green and blue
- The characteristic shape is rectangle
- The particular material is wood, paper
- The appropriate objects: wood items, plants and flowers, books, stripes, silk

Earth:

- A content element
- The specific colors are: brown, yellow, peach, and beige
- The characteristic shape is square
- The particular materials are bricks, stones, and ceramics
- The appropriate objects: tile, pottery, sand, rocks, marble, masonry

Metal:

- A content element

- The specific colors are: gray, silver, and white

- The characteristic shape is round

- The particular material is metal

- The appropriate objects: coins, metallic objects, rounded arches

Feng Shui has two important attributes: balance and harmony. To assure these attributes are effective for your environment, to balance yin and yang you can use the Five Elements.

It is of capital importance that all five elements are represented in your environment; if these elements are in equilibrium than your life will also be in equilibrium.

3.5 - BAGUA

BAGUA MAP

Wealth & Prosperity	Fame & Reputation	Love & Marriage
Health & Family	Spirituality	Creativity & Children
Wisdom & Knowledge	Career	Helpful People & Travel

The practitioners of Feng Shui developed an instrument called Bagua which is, in fact, a Feng Shui map. This map indicated where specific objects must be placed to improve the energy of that place.

They arranged their homes and workplaces in such a way as to bring good luck in the zones of: Travel & Helpful people, Children & Creativity, Romance & Relationships, Fame & Reputation, Wealth & Prosperity, Career & Path in life, Health, Family, Skills & Knowledge.

If we want to influence these zones in a room, we place the Bagua on the floor to locate them. If we need to balance the work we do over a desk, we place the Bagua on the desk and find the zones' arrangement. In this way, we can know how to bring good luck in specific zones which lack it.

There are 9-squares in a Bagua, and their position depends on the front door's position in your home.

In fact, Feng Shui Bagua (also named Pakua or Ba-Gua) is the map of any space and is the tool that analyzes the energy of that space.

Bagua literally means "eight zones".

There are two schools that somehow define Bagua in a different way.

A - The Classical or Traditional Feng Shui school

It makes a compass reading of your space. It is easy to define your Bagua if you have this compass reading and the floor plane of the space.

The nine Feng Shui zones of Bagua are:

1 - North (compass reading from 337.5 to 22.5 degrees)

Element: Water

Colors: Dark Blue and Black

Life Zone: Career & Path in Life

2 - Northeast (compass reading from 22.5 to 67.5 degrees)

Element: Earth

Colors: Black, Blue, Green

Life Zone: Wisdom & Knowledge

3 - East (compass reading from 67.5 to 112.5 degrees)

Element: Wood

Colors: Blue and Green

Life Zone: Health & Family

4 - Southeast (compass reading from 112.5 to 157.5 degrees)

Element: Wood

Colors: Blue, Purple, and Red

Life Zone: Wealth & Prosperity

5 - South (compass reading from 157.5 to 202.5 degrees)

Element: Fire

Colors: Red and Purple

Life Zone: Fame & Reputation

6 - Southwest (compass reading from 202.5 to 247.5 degrees)

Element: Earth

Colors: Pink, Red, and White

Life Zone: Love & Relationships

7 - West (compass reading from 247.5 to 292.5 degrees)

Element: Metal

Colors: White and Pastels

Life Zone: Creativity & Children

8 - Northwest (compass reading from 292.5 to 337.5 degrees)

Feng Shui Element: Metal

Colors: White, Black, and Gray

Life Zone: Helpful People & Travel

9 - Center

Feng Shui Element: Earth

Colors: Yellow, Orange, and Brown

Life Zone: Spirituality

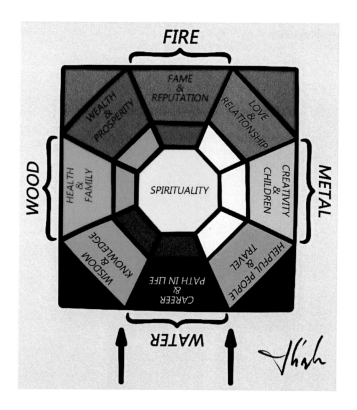

B - The Western Feng Shui school

It is also called the Modern school or Three Gates and targets the aspects of life, aligning Bagua with the front door of the house or office.

The door is taken as being the career section - the bottom center section of the Bagua map.

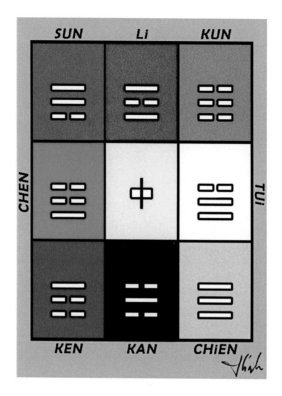

The nine sections of the Bagua of the Modern school are:

1 - Top row, left area: Wealth, Prosperity, Self-Worth

2 - Top row, center area: Fame, Reputation, Social Life

3 - Top row, right area: Marriage, Relationships, Partnerships

4 - Middle row, left area: Health, Family, Community

5 - Middle row, center area: Good Fortune, Well-being

6 - Middle row, right area: Children, Creativity, Entertainment

7 - Bottom row, left area: Wisdom, Self-Knowledge, Rest

8 - Bottom row, center area: Career, Life Mission, Individuality

9 - Bottom row, right area: Helpful People, Compassion, Travel

4
WHAT IS AN OFFICE?

4.1 - WHAT IS A FENG SHUI OFFICE?

First of all, let's define what an office is. You work. You have a job to do. For this, you need a place. No matter what the work description entails, to get the job done you need that special place called the office. An office is not necessarily a desk; nowadays it can have multiple forms: a studio, a car, a construction site... too many to try to mention all.

The main idea is that the place that you use to get the job done is called an office or working space.

The office is dependent on the person who is working there and also on the nature of the work that must be done. We will not mention the types of offices and what influences them; we will only talk about the office which our main character, the writer, is using to get his books, articles, and his work done.

The writer's productivity is directly related to his creativity. And his creativity is related with the harmony in his working place. This harmony can be defined in many variants, but we will say for now that harmony is when you feel happy when all is coming together. Saying this, we must understand that a writer can find this harmony in several places, not only sitting at a desk. But speaking about an office, we will refer from now on to the room that the writer is using to finalize his projects, the writing of the final product.

To find the harmony in his writing place, the writer needs to apply the productivity principles combined with a design and layout that is suitable for the nature of the writing process.

And here are the steps in the ancient art of Feng Shui. The writer's Chi has to find a balance that will influence his creativity each moment. Depending on the field of interest in which the writer is working in, there can be various solutions to control the flowing Chi.

This book doesn't intend to address the writer's work or artistic skills but rather it addresses each writing category. We have to do this because what is harmony for a romantic novel writer is different than what is harmony for a journalist writer, and for sure very different than for the writer writing for the horror domain.

You already got the idea. To bring the Feng Shui technique into the writer's life, it is not enough to merely explain general principles and ideas; we have to dig deeper because the branches of writing are so numerous.

Except when applying the combination between the principles of productivity and the design of the office, we must pay important attention to what is called the functionality of the office.

A proper office helps you be productive and feel inspired, and when it is done well, Feng Shui will boost them and bring success your way.

By applying Feng Shui in your writing life, you will learn to de-clutter your office, to organize it, to use artwork to balance the Chi flow, to harmonize your space choosing the right colors, plants, light and many others which will incorporate stress relievers in such a manner so you will easily achieve your goals.

Using the yin and yang balance or the Feng Shui elements, we will learn step by step how to balance and harmonize our office. It doesn't matter what system you choose to use. All that matters is to choose what you feel is right for you to achieve harmony and creativity while maintaining a boost of inspiration.

4.2 - ORGANIZING YOUR WRITING PLACE

Sometimes, we as writers find ourselves in a total unorganized space. We don't remember the steps that we made to arrive at this point but still, if we look around us, it seems that everything is a big mess. And at a subconscious level this mess influences the harmony inside our brains, the tranquility and peace inside our hearts and, for this reason, our writing is also influenced in a negative way.

Our lives will be easier if each needed object we utilize is in the right place so we would only need to raise our hands to reach them, without losing time in trying to find what we need.

Imagine a situation in which you are writing. Your creativity suddenly reaches a maximum level, and the words are flowing like a beautiful river. You remember that in order to finish, you need the note you took some time ago suitable for what you are now writing.

You raise your hand to reach the note but... the note is not there... you know you had it... but now it's not there... you start to search for it;

"What a mess I have on my desk! Where is that note? I know I had it here! Where can it be?" you are talking to yourself while looking for what you need. Maybe soon, you will find it, or maybe it will take a longer time... but meanwhile... meanwhile, the flow of your words is now blocked. You added to the path of this flow a stressing situation, a blockage that will influence your work.

At this moment, you need some time to readjust your mind, your heart and your all, to what you were writing. The result will not be the same as before, and your productivity will have to suffer. And what is the reason for all that's happened? For the only reason that your desk, your office, your writing place was not properly organized.

Nothing is more counterproductive and frustrating than wasting your time and blocking the flow of your words, wasting time to find the tools that you needed. Make it a point to designate a special place for each device you know you need while you are writing. Try to maintain this place and next time when you need the object placed there, your creativity and productivity will not suffer the blows.

You have to understand that the state of your desk is a reflection of your work, and the state of your work is a reflection of your desk. They are so interdependent and if you want one of them to be positively influenced than you have to take care of the other one also. This interdependence determines the success of your writing career.

Clean your desk of clutter and let the Chi flow freely to allow you to be inspired, to have new ideas and to feel powerful in your office. Everything that you need must be within arm's reach. You don't need to stand up and walk around the room to find a needed item.

All that you need when you are writing is to sit in the writer's chair and write. Finally, a writer writes!

4.3 - DESIGN YOUR WRITING SPACE TO ACHIEVE YOUR GOALS

If we are in the beginning stage of arranging our office, we should first design the layout, so we will not need to do anything afterward.

Many people, when they hear the word office, are instantly thinking of a desk and a computer. But this is not so. An office is that space where our job is done. It includes the desk and the surroundings also. So, to have a Feng Shui office, we first need to design it if this was not already done.

The design must be simple and manageable and in the writer's case it should include a desk, a chair and for sure a bookcase. These are the main elements. Of course, we can have other things also as decorations but the basics for a writer are these three things.

When we design our writing office, we should keep in mind that the design must show anyone the intention of writing in that space.

A traditional office space is designed in a Yang style. This means we have an open space with plenty of excess room to freely promote moving chi residing within the office space. No matter whether the office will be at home or not, we should always think about it as a tool that helps us accomplish our goals, meaning a high quality written book, article or whatever we write.

If our office is placed in our home, tuning it to complement our personality is a must.

The goal is to keep the right balance of Yin and Yang to match the purpose of your office with your personality and habits.

The room that we will choose to write in should be one where the sunlight can freely enter and where we can have lots of foot traffic. If by chance outside the building, in front of the office window is a water element, this will have a positive effect on our writing. But we must be aware to have a living water element and not a motionless one. In the case of stagnant water, in time, the energies of that place will cause financial difficulties and health problems. And... what writer would want to write without having an income or having a poor state of health.

If we can see from our window a mountain that is too close, then we will face obstacles in our publishing process. But if the mountain is far enough, this will bring us protection, which is a very good thing. Avoid the buildings with Sha Chi (Chi provided by sharp corners, sharp roofs, square buildings, and pillars). In case that we already possess the house and don't want to move, Feng Shui provides us the tools that we need to get rid of the Sha Chi problems.

The Sha Chi is the negative side of Chi, also called the "killing Chi" and can be natural or manmade. When we meet a natural Sha Chi, even if it is a Chi trapped on the surface or below the surface of our location, it is better if we could relocate. This kind of Sha Chi is very hard to negate or overcome unless you can find the real cause for it. Sometimes this can only be the radiance from some rocks nearby, or maybe we have an underground cave that stocks the energy.

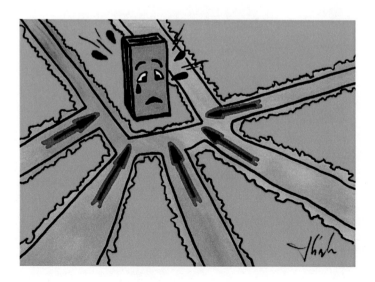

This can be somehow fixed if moving is not an option. But if the natural Sha Chi is caused by the past suffering of the people who lived in those places, it is preferable to move. There are very few people who can handle and heal this type of a Sha Chi situation.

When we are talking about man-made Sha Chi, this is usually caused by clutter that blocks the flow of Chi and makes it stagnant. The solution is to clean the clutter. Don't take it and put in another location; you will only succeed to change its place, but the problem would still be around your office.

Another example of Sha Chi is the effect given by what we call "the poison arrow." This is provoked by sharp objects (a wall is also considered an object) which have corners directly across from where you sit. If the poison arrow is interior, Feng Shui recommends positioning a large plant in front of the sharp corner or a multifaceted crystal near us which will disperse the Sha Chi coming towards us.

If the poison arrow is an external one directed at our building, then the remedy is to place a Feng Shui Bagua mirror in its direction, which cures the effect of the arrow. This kind of exterior Sha Chi is produced by square buildings, walls, pillars, telephone poles, bridges, cemeteries, and roads, which point these poison arrows towards your home.

Until now, we talked about designing your office according with the external environment. Even if we succeed to arrange the inside office in accordance with Feng Shui principles, we must also be aware of the external influences that are affecting our writing mood and the final product of our work.

Speaking about designing the interior of our writing space, we have to be aware of some particular situations that help the Chi flow. Some of this advice will be further divulged in future subchapters.

To have a truly peaceful and tranquil area for our creativity, it would be great if the back of our office would be positioned in the wealth corner of Bagua. Our desk should always be placed in a position to see the door, so any movement from that direction is known, but still not put us in line with the door. You have to also place the desk without facing a wall. Seems to be complicated but if you would take into consideration all the possible locations for the desk, you will for sure find a position. And if this is not possible, Feng Shui will provide you remedies also.

An office with large windows is very good for Chi flow but if we don't have windows, we can fix this by hanging a painting depicting water or a garden scene on the wall.

If you intend to invite your writing partners inside your office, even if it is at home or not, consider having it towards the front of the house. This is very important for the future of your business. Never forget, a writer who writes and has an office where he is doing this, it is said that he also has a business, and so the office and the building represent the writer's business. We will talk more about this later.

Here we only mentioned the best design needed for our office to achieve our dreams. If we do this, our subconscious mind will always receive reinforcement and will direct us to act accordingly in our work.

4.4 - DECORATING THE WRITER'S OFFICE

After we have decided and designed the home office or the outside office space, we have to also take into consideration the decorations. This is a great challenge and requires various resources.

Each addition should increase the productivity and positively influence the creativity of the writer. No matter what decorations we need and choose, to make the Chi freely flow, we must always pay attention to the state they are in. If, at a specific moment in time we notice that a decoration was damaged or broken, we must immediately remove it, no matter of the initial power and influence that it had. Any malfunctioning and broken decoration will place obstacles between us as writers and the goals that we have. This will make us lose time, and time is one of the most valuable resources that we have.

We have to incorporate the right balance between Yin and Yang so to match them with our personality, work habits and writing goals.

The decorations that we should always use must inspire and speak to us about abundance, prosperity, success... in a few words, everything that we want to accomplish. For this, we can hang images, mottos, pictures and symbols.

In the writing space, we can place some family photos but we have to be careful with this aspect. Too many family photos in your office will attract the energy of your children or parents, and this will distract and interrupt you from your work.

Being decorative also, the furniture that we will choose for our writing space must talk to us about an abundance, prosperity, creativity, etc.

Don't face an empty wall. Decorate it, or else you will always have a feeling that you face obstacles, and this will bring you a lack of vision and perception, as well as make you lose different opportunities. Make sure you have a pleasant view while sitting at your desk. Surround yourself with things that inspire your creativity. Start listening to your heart and add in your environment whatever it's telling you that you need. Don't be worried that your heart hasn't yet read about the ancient technique of Feng Shui. I am telling you... your heart already is a Feng Shui expert. But if you still don't trust in it, use your brain also while reading this book or other books in this field. Step by step, you will understand and feel what you always knew.

And speaking of what you know... you probably already know this, but remember to always choose furniture with round corners for your office. If somehow you already have furniture that has sharp corners, at least pay attention to place it out of the flow of traffic.

As decorations, you can add music instruments and even sounds (yes... we can look at sounds as decorations also). Add running water, burn some incense, generally speaking, try to transform your writing place into a sacred temple where you can always refuge, far away from the ordinary world.

About colors, we will have a different chapter, so we will not speak about them here. Colors are vitally important for a writer's life, and choosing a color depends a lot on the writer's area of interest. But keep in mind that colors belong to the decoration field, and they play a very important role in it.

Add flowers also, and your world will suddenly be transformed into a magic garden. Surround the harsh angles of the furniture with plants. We will also have a chapter only for plants, so we will not dig into this theme here. But we have to admit… what more beautiful decoration can there be for an office than a living plant?

Decorate the office with sculptures; they will sure absorb the negativity from your working place.

If we want to write novels, we have to place bookshelves with classic novels and modern books in our working space as well. Place on your desktop pens and a picture with a writing activity. You can hang on walls, or you can frame a book cover with your name as an author on your desk.

If you are a lyricist or a librettist, place scenes with musical themes on your desk or hang them on your walls. The Chi created by these decorations will influence your creativity.

Every object in your office has an influence on you. The relation between people, places, and things is called Numinosity. Literally speaking, this concept is formed by two words: Numen (defined as a spiritual force of a natural place, phenomenon or object) and Numinous (described as supernatural and mysterious force which appeals to the higher emotions and has influence over people).

A living office decorated in accordance with the Feng Shui's principles, is inviting you to write, invites your working partners to have prolific conversations, and make all who enter feel comfortable; and by the way… the first one who's entering there is you.

There are cases when the structural design of your office doesn't allow you to decorate according with the obvious Feng Shui principles. In this case you shouldn't despair; Feng Shui has alternative methods to overcome any obstacle. Decorative objects like mirrors, chimes, fountains and crystals will allow the Chi to flow, so your creativity, mind comfort and abundance in the writing process will receive the needed boost.

So, try to understand the numinosity born between you and your writing space and make sure that your office has an uplifting influence on you!

4.5 - TIPS FOR WRITING AT HOME; ROOM DIVIDERS

There are many benefits to working at home, but there are also lots of obstacles.

Feng Shui is about maintaining balance, and for sure a balance between work and family life must also be kept.

In the particular case in which we prefer to place our office in our home, we need to pay lots of attention on separating our working life from the family life. This separation can be easily made by what we call room dividers.

These room dividers physically separate our working place as much as possible. This is needed because we will have moments when we want our office to be felt like a refuge in which we can create our books or writing pieces.

The office should be separate from any other area of our home so that we can concentrate on our job.

It is easy to do this if we have a separate room as our office. But what should we do if the configuration of our home doesn't allow us to have this separate space?

In the case where we have a shared room, we must create a sense of privacy using screens and curtains.

It is preferable not to place our office in the bedroom. But if we have to do it, a room divider is necessary. Except for screens, another good room divider is placing a large rug to mark off our home office. If we can build a raised platform for our desk, this would be even better, and the screens or curtains would not be necessary anymore.

Another room divider that we can use even if it sounds somehow weird is… our attitude. Yes, our attitude is a very good room divider. For example, whenever we write we shut the door. This is related with a strict discipline that we have to maintain, and we have to teach the rest of the family to respect it.

If closing the door is not possible, use a curtain to screen off your view from being able to see the rest of the house. This will help the writer concentrate on what he is doing and avoid distractions from the family's daily life.

Keep a strict attitude also when it is about setting up the office hours. You are the first one who must respect this, so the rest of the family members will also respect it.

Another room divider for the case where you have a shared room for your writing job is to use a separate phone line in the working space. This will enable your subconscious mind to believe that your office is exactly what it's supposed to be… your writing office.

While you are working during the already scheduled time-frame, dress properly and never remain in the clothes that you normally wear around the house. This attitude will enhance your Chi.

Never use the dining room table as your desk. In the long term, this will ruin your writing career because your mind will never be able to concentrate on the writing aspect as long as your family problems will keep your attention busy.

For a physical separation, you can use bookcases and shelves with doors made of wood or any other opaque material. You can also use open shelves but only if they don't direct their corners towards your body as to create poison arrows in your workspace.

As we mentioned, there are several benefits in choosing to work from home. On the one hand, we have the freedom to choose our working hours. On the other hand, we are free of any influence associated with commercial buildings (lights, electromagnetic fields, poor air quality, etc.)

All these conditions we have at home help us increase the creativity and productivity.

Arrange your desk and workspace so that a solid wall is behind you and the door is in front of you. In front of your desk there should be more open space than behind it; in this way the Chi will flow freely. If you have no way of facing the door, and you must have your desk where your back will be towards the door's direction, you can cure this situation by placing a mirror in front of your desk, so your eyes can observe the door behind you at any moment.

In the space designated for the writing activity, decorate the walls with objects that remind you of your writing goals; don't use any artwork objects suitable for other rooms in your home.

Never eat your meals, read other books except for what your job requires or watch television in your workplace.

Because you don't have any coworkers to disturb, you can play your favorite music you feel will stimulate your creativity. Place plants and moving water near your desk. No one is there to tell you that you're not allowed.

One of the greatest advantages of working at home is the ability to use your home objects: chairs, desks, lamps, etc. However, try to avoid adding too many objects into your home office. It is better to keep the place open for the Chi flow. Excessive amount of objects will clutter your space, and your productivity will be influenced by this.

A simple design assures the success of a home office.

The Chi flow can be increased by using earth, fire and metal Feng Shui elements in the home office. Feel free to express your creativity through the decorations you choose for your working space but use them wisely.

Pay proper attention to the Fame and Reputation areas by placing them in a Southern direction, which are characterized by the Fire element. Remember to never use water elements (blue color, big mirrors, and fountains) in this space because water elements put down the fire energy. To have a great reputation as a writer, use any fire element in this area.

Your Career as a writer is represented by the North direction. The specific Feng Shui elements for this area are Water and Metal. In this space, place elements that symbolize water and metal.

The area of Prosperity and Abundance is the Southeast direction. Here you must place images that symbolize money. You can very well place photos with books, as many of your published books as possible so that it will influence your productivity. The Feng Shui element necessarily in this area is Wood. So, keep in mind to avoid Fire and Metal elements here. They will damage the abundance of your writing pieces and your selling phase.

Even if you chose to have your office at home, we already know that everything is connected on the energy level, so you must Feng Shui your working space so you can build a successful home-based writing enterprise.

4.6 - TIPS FOR WRITING AT YOUR OUTSIDE OFFICE

To attract success in your writing career, you must also take care of your outside office space in order to create a Feng Shui environment. It would be great if your co-workers would agree with the remedies that you will need to apply for the Chi to flow freely. In case that the relations between you are not so close, and they don't agree, try to Feng Shui your section of the office as much as possible.

For your desk, choose a powerful position in which you'll have a perfect view of the door. Also behind you, try to have a solid wall and not a window. If the configuration of your office doesn't permit this, add plants on the window side so it will build an artificial wall. If your co-workers have already occupied the powerful position for the desk and yours can't face the door, place a mirror on your desk oriented towards the door's direction.

If you have sharp corners that throw poison arrows in your direction, mask them with large plants or place crystals there.

Apply the Bagua to your office and chose the best remedies for particular situations.

Don't forget to periodically de-clutter your working section. Give space for the Chi to flow.

Try to select your desk according with your personality and your writing type. If for example, you are a journalist and your style is to be very imaginative, then to bring you back to earth, you can use an earth aligned desk, a sturdy desk and a flat, large desktop on it.

If your personality is "down to earth" but you work for a fantasy periodical or a Romantic based magazine, you can choose a narrow desk surrounded by bookshelves.

For a writer, no matter what type of writing he's doing, metallic desks, which can get too cold should be avoided; wooden desks are preferable, as they will boost the writer's creativity.

Keep everything that you usually use on the desk within arm's reach. It is more comfortable, and you won't lose precious time finding an object, especially knowing that your writing mood can leave you.

The rest of the advice you received for the home office setup remains valuable for the outside office space also, but, of course, try not to start a conflict with your co-workers. The worst clutter that you can have in your working office is to have a discordant atmosphere towards your colleagues.

4.7 - FURNITURE FOR YOUR OFFICE

The best case is when you work from home, and you can choose your furniture without any restriction from another co-worker or employer.

Choose stylish wood desks and forget about the metal cabinets that are often used in an office.

The most important piece in your Feng Shui office is your chair. If you can't afford a brand new chair, then try to find one that was used by a successful predecessor. Never use a chair that belonged to someone who was fired or who failed in his writing career.

If you buy a new chair be careful, many of them don't respect the Feng Shui principles. Try to find only those which can help and will protect you.

Buy a solid based one, so it has stability in your writing career and to not meet each moment with a writer's block. Look for a chair that has armrests, which symbolize support and protection.

A Feng Shui chair is one that has a solid back, which does not have a gap between the back and the seat. Also, you must always remember that the height of your chair's back is influencing the success in your career as a writer. If it's not possible to possess a chair whose back reaches to your head level, you must at least choose one that comes up to your shoulder's level.

A Feng Shui secret that few know is to place small pieces of plastic or wood buffers under your desk to raise it a few inches. Do the same with your chair and raise it according with the new desk's position. You will notice in a short time how new opportunities will come your way.

5
THE WRITER'S DESK

5.1 - POSITIONING THE DESK - THE COMMANDER

OK… you are a writer, and you decided to have an office.

Let's take a detailed look together on how we can Feng Shui your working place.

The desk… is the most important furniture for a writer; of course together with the chair you use.

Regarding Feng Shui and your desk, first of all you have to find a place for it. This is the place where you will spend all your working days; this is the place where you will write. Doing this, using it daily and keeping its location unchanged attracts seriosity towards you and making your writing a priority.

Until now we talked about our office being placed at home or having an official one. However, there is another situation that we haven't mentioned yet but let's do it now to be sure that we don't forget anything.

It is the situation which some writers prefer... writing in public places like coffee shops. What is Feng Shui say regarding a technique for this? Well... it is saying almost nothing because this situation is not in your hands. If the owner of that public place knows how to Feng Shui it, it's fine... fine for you. If not, then there is nothing you can do. The only choice you have is to use or not to use that space as your office. For sure this is not my style. I personally prefer the privacy of my home office.

So, even if in that situation you can't choose where to place your desk, you still have all the liberty in your personal office, no matter where you decided for it to be.

The most important statement that we can make regarding this is to always place your desk in what we call "the command position". It is named this because it appoints you most "in command".

This position has the base roots in our desire and instinctive tendency to have visible control of what's around us. As humans, we feel the need to control and check out what's new; we don't like too many surprises, and that's also the case in our office.

This command position gives us the opportunity to see the entry to our office. As writers, we have to deal with multiple situations of suspense which we need to include in our books. These situations, even if they are imaginative, are dragging our attention inside of them and while we are writing about them, we practically participate in the action with our hearts; because this is the sign of a good writer, isn't it?

So, it would be very distracting for a writer to be in any other position than the commander, and to always have to worry about what is happening behind his back. For sure the quality of the writing process would not be so productive.

The creativity would not flow freely or be used to its fullest potential as long as your concentration is split on several things at the same time and most of all… one of these things being something to really worry about. In a nutshell, as writers we need to be in control of our world.

The ideal commander position is when sitting on our chair, we can directly view the door but not directly be aligned with the door, to also be able to see the window and to have behind our back a solid wall. Another variant of the commander position is to see it all using our peripheral sight. But if we can choose the ideal one, on a long term basis it will be the best choice for our career.

If the space that you have doesn't allow you to do this, you can Feng Shui the position of your desk by placing a mirror on it in which case you can now perfectly view the entrance to your office.

Check the position of your desk now. Is it exactly as what we mentioned above? If yes, then good for you; you are on the right track! If no, start to change it. Think, design and apply these recommendations; take command of your job and notice what will happen in your career.

Now, don't forget about your chair. It also belongs to the commander position so choose it carefully. The best chair is the high-backed one, which doesn't have any gaps between the seat and the back. Choose it so that the backrest comes up at least to your shoulder's level.

If by chance, you have to share your office with a coworker, try to avoid the back to back position of the desk and also the face to face one. Both of these situations generate conflicts. If you can't avoid these situations because it is not in your hands, then cure them by adding a plant between you and your coworker.

If you can place the desk facing the door but realize you have a window behind you, place many plants in the window, and this will provide you stability again.

It is very important that you view and examine your room by sitting at your desk. So, even if you are facing the door, try to also avoid seeing blank walls. This will bring you a lack of vision and opportunities; a writer needs to have vision as much as he needs to breathe. So, decorate the wall according with Feng Shui principles by adding vibrant bright artwork that symbolizes writing opportunities for you.

Once you feel and understand how it is to be sitting in the commander position, you will start to notice that you instinctively look after it wherever you have to go in public spaces, at business meetings, etc.

To be in this commander position doesn't mean that you are other people's commander. It means you are in control of your own energy so you can do your best in any situation you are involved in.

5.2 - DE-CLUTTERING THE DESK

We need a special subchapter for this issue because this is one of the most important aspects when we Feng Shui an office and, generally speaking, any space.

It is imperative to maintain an uncluttered working space when writing. We already know that our subconscious mind has a strong connection with the environment we are working in, so our mind is directly influenced by what's around us. If we want to keep a clear mind, to increase our productivity by boosting our creativity, we need an uncluttered desk.

To unclutter a desk doesn't only mean cleaning it by dusting. It also means not storing too many things on it, even if they are needed; they have their position in other places. Don't keep excessive equipment, files and paperwork on your desk. Find another place for them near you and free your desk of what's unnecessary. Don't auto sabotage your potential opportunities having a cluttered desk.

This clutter situation has a strong impact not only on your mind but also on your emotional, physical and spiritual well-being states. When you unclutter your working space, you bring in vital Chi that helps your clarity, creativity, focus, and comfort.

A clutter free desk allows you to have refreshing ideas and energy. This will increase your effectiveness and productivity, will attract abundance to you, will reduce the stress that you work with, and will also give you space for new projects.

To unclutter the desk also means to pay attention to any wires and cords, and to hide them as much as possible.

The area under your desk also belongs to your working place so keep it clean and free of clutter. Maintain enough free space there so you can stretch your legs whenever you feel the need to do it. There is a very interesting fact that was noticed regarding this. Stretching your body also stretches your mind, and this is very good for your creative process.

A psychological fact is that if you store many things under your desk, you will feel stuck, and this will affect your writing process also. As a result, your career as a writer will be influenced in a negative way.

To unclutter your desk also means to get rid of everything you don't use or love. Because everything is energy and energy attracts things in your life, getting rid of objects you don't love is a very important step for your health. These objects bring down your energy level, and this low level will cause health problems after a while.

As a conclusion, don't think about this too much. Get rid of the clutter on your desk! Clean it having the permanent intention of clearing away the old and acquiring free space for new opportunities to come into your life.

Do it and observe how your life as a writer will change!

5.3 - SIZE, SHAPE, MATERIALS FOR YOUR DESK

When we choose our desk, we have to pay attention to these elements also.

Of course our preference here has a very important role. Whatever makes us feel comfortable will boost the Chi around us and balance our minds.

According with these preferences, we will choose the size of our desk so we can place on it all the objects and equipment we think necessary for our writing process. I personally prefer an adequate size, able to include my laptop, a small shelve for my documents and daily notes, some object to hold my writing instruments, my phone devices, and of course having enough free spaces to move my hands.

Possessing a desk with a roll out drawer for a keyboard, but only utilizing my laptop and not a standard computer, I am able to use this drawer to keep some more handy personal documents and notes that I would need daily. So, this too provides me some extra free space on the desk.

Even if having a very large desk sounds nice, I advise you not to choose one, at least not so large where you can't reach with your arm's length the needed objects. It is not necessary to struggle by reaching for something needed and not being able to grab it without moving your body. If the desk is too big, even if you placed it in the commander position, or even if its size makes you look like you conquered the world, soon it will make you feel like you lost control and authority; for the simple fact that you can't reach the items that you need.

Regarding the shapes that we can have for our desk, here we can mention the following situations:

- A curved shape desk is very good for concentration, but only in the situation in which you are sitting on the inside of the curves, so the energy is pulled towards you.

- A rectangular desk will increase your concentration.

- A desk with circular shape is ideal for brainstorming and creativity.

- A desk with a closed front establishes boundaries; it can make you feel protected.

- A desk with an open front gives others a more comfortable feeling when they approach you.

The Feng Shui materials used for a desk and their influence are:

- Wood: brings predictability and support in our life and also gives a long lasting solid feeling.

- Metal: keeps alive our concentration and mental energy.

- Laminate: energetically neutral.

- Glass: gives others the sensation that you have nothing to hide but for you this is not such a comfortable situation because the energy moves too fast around you.

5.4 - FENG SHUI YOUR DESK

To Feng Shui your desk, it means to arrange physical objects on it in such a way as to attract positive energy towards you and your writing activity. This arrangement will affect the flow of Chi within the space, and if the Chi is good, we will receive a boost of positive energy.

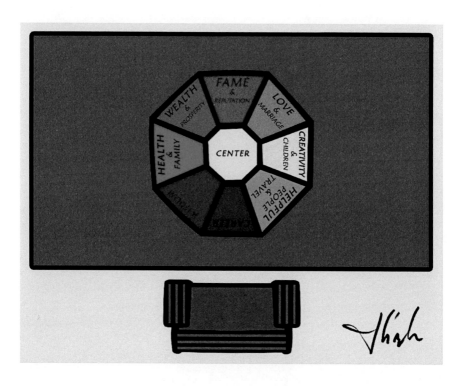

A Feng Shui practitioner has one basic tool, and this is the Bagua Map. Details about this map can be found in subchapter 5.5 of this book. Here we will try to apply this map for each category of writers.

Before placing the Feng Shui remedies that will boost the energy for specific domains of writing in each area, check again if the desk is cluttered. If so, then anything that is unfinished, unresolved, and disorganized must be taken off to free the area for allowing the Chi flow.

When you use the Bagua map, place the bottom, meaning the Knowledge & Wisdom, Career & Life Path, Travel & Helpful People row, in the area where you sit.

Let's now take a look at each area to see how we can Feng Shui it:

1. Wealth & Prosperity

- The rear left corner of the desk represents Prosperity and Wealth.

- You can add here a green plant (especially a bamboo) or a crystal to attract money and abundance.

- The computer can also be placed here with very good results for your prosperity.

- A clean running fountain placed in this corner will maintain a high self-esteem.

- A lava lamp in this area will give you energy for your work.

- Category of writers who should concentrate more on this square: obviously all writers should take care of this corner: poets, novelists, satirists, lyricists, librettists, playwrights, speechwriters, screenwriters, biographers, critics, editors, encyclopedists, essayist, lexicographers, historians, researchers, scholars, translators, bloggers, diarists, journalists, columnists, memoirists, letter writers, ghostwriters, technical writers, scribes, report writers, writers of sacred texts.

2. Fame & Reputation

- If you want to be in the spotlight, you have to concentrate in the center-back of the Bagua map.

- It is useful here to place business cards or your nameplate (if you chose to use a Pen name, write it on this plate).

- You can also place anything that motivates you (a diploma or a photo from your past where you won a contest).

- Keep this area very clean. If you place the monitor here, choose an image for your screen that emotionally gives you power and recognition.

- A lamp is also well placed here.

- Category of writers who should concentrate more on this square: almost all writers should take care of this area (exceptions are ghost writers, letter writers, and scribes): poets, novelists, satirists, lyricists, librettists, playwrights, speechwriters, screenwriters, biographers, critics, editors, encyclopedists, essayist, lexicographers, historians, researchers, scholars, translators, bloggers, diarists, journalists, columnists, memoirists, technical writers, report writers, writers of sacred texts.

3. Love & Relationships

- To have harmonious relationships with your editors, agents, publishers, readers focus on the back-right corner.

- It is a good choice placing your computer in this area, but be careful that the computer isn't broken because it will cancel its influence.

- You can also place a photo of a happy couple or two red roses here.

- Category of writers who should concentrate more on this square: all writers should take care of this corner: poets, novelists, satirists, lyricists, librettists, playwrights, speechwriters, screenwriters, biographers, critics, editors, encyclopedists, essayist, lexicographers, historians, researchers, scholars, translators, bloggers, diarists, journalists, columnists, memoirists, letter writers, ghostwriters, technical writers, scribes, report writers, writers of sacred texts.

- If you write romance novels, love poems, love lyrics, romantic screenwriting's and romantic librettos, paying more attention to this corner will even double the success rate for you.

4. Creativity & Children

- If you are an aspiring writer, you can fill this area like your own home.

- Put a journal or a book in the right center of the grid. A blank sketchbook would be ideal, or a metal object may work well for all writers.

- In this area, it is also good to place pens, markers and scissors.

- Category of writers who should concentrate more on this square: all writers should take care of this area: poets, novelists, satirists, lyricists, librettists, playwrights, speechwriters, screenwriters, biographers, critics, editors, encyclopedists, essayist, lexicographers, historians, researchers, scholars, translators, bloggers, diarists, journalists, columnists, memoirists, letter writers, ghostwriters, technical writers, scribes, report writers, writers of sacred texts.

- If you write books for children, if you're just thinking of becoming a writer, or if you are a scholar and a researcher, you must take care of this area because for you, it will double boost the creativity.

5. Helpful People and Travel

- Focus on the front-right section if the subject that you write about is based on compassion or travels.

- Add in this area a phone, a travel guide or an address book.

- You can also place a photo of a dream vacation.

- Category of writers who should concentrate more on this square: poets, novelists, historians, diarists, journalists, columnists, report writers, writers of sacred texts.

6. Career & Path in life

- Front-center must be kept free of clutter.

- It is good if you display motivational affirmations in this area.

- Also, the computer would be well placed here.

- Category of writers who should concentrate more on this square: all writers should take care of this area: poets, novelists, satirists, lyricists, librettists, playwrights, speechwriters, screenwriters, biographers, critics, editors, encyclopedists, essayist, lexicographers, historians, researchers, scholars, translators, bloggers, diarists, journalists, columnists, memoirists, letter writers, ghostwriters, technical writers, scribes, report writers, writers of sacred texts.

- If you are a biographer, historian, diarist, memoirist writer of sacred texts, you have to pay double attention to this area because you will receive back more.

7. Knowledge and Wisdom

- Focus on the front-left corner of the desk if you learn or study, or if you write about these issues.

- You can place in this area a reference book for your field of interest.

- Category of writers who should concentrate more on this

square: speechwriters, critics, editors, encyclopedists, essayist, lexicographers, historians, researchers, scholars, translators, technical writers, report writers, writers of sacred texts.

8. Family & Health

- To Feng Shui this area, you have to place a happy family photo in the left-center of the desk. You can place this photo in a wood frame, or if you already have your computer in this space, you can add it on your computer's desktop.

- Category of writers who should concentrate more on this square: novelists, lyricists, librettists, playwrights, screenwriters, biographers, historians, diarists, columnists, memoirists, technical writers, report writers (especially if you are a technical medical writer or a medical report writer).

9. Spirituality

- The center area of your desk must be kept clean of clutter.

- Category of writers who should concentrate more on this square: all writers should take care of this space.

As a general advice, the Chinese Feng Shui masters suggest keeping a glass of water on your desk. Depending on the area in which you place it, the energy will receive a positive boost, and you will increase your abilities according with the specific square on your Bagua map.

Still, it is preferable to keep the glass of water on the left or right side and to avoid the center, center-back and center-front areas.

Any water that you place near your desk or on your desk collects the negative energy. This will help you maintain your health being and will give you a boost of creativity so you can become more productive.

Don't forget to hide and tape the wires that you have near you. You don't need a mess on your desk.

If your desk has drawers, note that these are also very important for your writing career. Keep them uncluttered and organized.

Clean your computer regularly, inside and outside, including the desktop's contents.

From now on, try to look at your desk like it's a small universe that is influencing your life. If you really wish to smooth your path and let the Chi flow to boost each domain in your life, then one of the main things you must do is pay attention to your desk where you write your books and articles.

5.5 - FENG SHUI BACKING

Feng Shui backing means to act in such way that good energy is always behind your back.

This is necessary while you are writing so your conscious mind receives a peaceful feeling and lets you work with a comfortable sensation.

To achieve good Feng Shui backing, you must have a solid wall behind your back. If you placed some shelves on this wall, it would be very good to add a decorative Tortoise that will give you the energy of one of the four Feng Shui animals.

The best option is to have a turtle living in an aquarium behind you.

If the wall behind your back is not solid, you can remedy this by adding an image of a mountain on it.

Even if we already talked about your chair, we have to mention it here again because, for good Feng Shui backing, your chair must have a solid high backrest without any gaps.

Be aware not to have any poison arrows pointing to your back. In this case, you must somehow place a Feng Shui mirror between your back and the source of the Shar Chi. If you don't have any other possibility of placement then hang the mirror on the back of your chair.

If behind your back you somehow have a window, place several plants in that area that will have the role of a wall which will protect you.

5.6 - CUBICLE FENG SHUI

When the configuration of your office and the rest of the furniture you have included are obliging you to design a Cubicle desk, you have to pay special attention to some elements.

A cubicle design is a powerful way to transform your working place into an area in which your creativity, productivity, and abundance are totally boosted.

Unfortunately, many possessors of cubicle desks don't know how they can bring remedies to this situation and, for this reason, the negative energy is flowing freely, influencing their lives.

In fact, any objects, event or situation can influence us in a supportive way or a damaging one. All we need is to have some knowledge about what's happening and to bring cures to those issues. So, any harming source can be transformed into a loving and sacred situation.

It's easier to Feng Shui a cubicle desk if we decided to write in our home office.

In the case where we are official employees and the employer decides how to arrange the desks in a cubicle style, this can bring bad Feng Shui to our work. Many times, the cubicle desks from such an office create barriers without shelters; energetically poisoned arrows are directed at the writer, and often has limited access to sunlight.

To Feng Shui such a desk, we need to do some minor changes that will not cause any irritation to anyone.

1. If we can't place the desk in the commander position, it is necessary to place a mirror on it, to always see what is happening behind us and you will never feel energetically attacked or anxious.

- If your employers don't allow you to add a mirror to the environment, you can obtain a similar effect with a metallic object that will reflect the door's view.

2. Never forget to un-clutter the desk.

- There is no acceptable reason to block more of the good energy in a cubicle situation.

- Get rid of everything that you don't need.

3. Add plants to your desk especially in the areas that need it.

- In cubicle Feng Shui, plants are essential because they reject negative energy and soften any sharp corner or edges.

- Your soul will feel nourished if you choose the plants well.

4. Be sure that you have proper lighting, and if not, add a lamp to cure this issue.

- Adding a supplementary light source to a cubicle desk is always better.

- Choose a nice lamp that will decorate your environment.

- The light will activate Chi, and it will stimulate the clarity with which you need to write.

5. Decorate, balance and harmonize your cubicle desk like it is your own home to give you a comfortable feeling.

- Color your cubicle world and don't let the lack of colors block the Chi flow.

- Try to calm the yang, which is preponderant for a cubicle

desk. For this, rest assured that the metal and earth elements are mixed with fire and water to create the necessary equilibrium.

- Transform your cubicle desk into a place where you feel alive, so your writing creativity and productivity will be boosted.

- Wallpaper your cubicle and be creative with this part.

- Use beautiful images from nature, which will make you feel relaxed.

6. If you write at your home office you can add several Feng Shui remedies to your cubicle, but if you share your office with other co-workers, you'll have to Feng Shui it in a subtle way.

- Don't try to hang wind chimes, Bagua mirrors and three legged frogs.

- People will look at you in a weird way.

- If you can decorate your cubicle with wallpaper, place a framed colored happy photo on your desk.

6
THE WRITER'S INNER WORLD

6.1 - THE WRITER'S BLOCK

You are a writer! Do you remember the moment when you decided to be a writer? You were so emotional, so full of energy, happy and anxious to finish writing your first novel, or maybe a series of great articles or whatever you decided to write.

At that moment, you felt that the world would fall at your feet with the release of your first book. You already imagined how the words would flow to create gorgeous materials with your pen (or maybe your keyboard).

You started to write... and you wrote... and you wrote... and BANG!!! Something suddenly happened!

Your computer is in front of you, the cursor is blinking, your brain is totally blocked and you are staring at a blank screen. You suddenly understand what you never admitted could happen to you has in fact just happened.

You are completely, totally immersed in that weird, abyssal level called a Writer's Block!!!

You are there, but you still don't understand how it was possible for this to happen to you. It can happen to others, of course... but to you?

After the first moment of shock, you realize that it's real and there for you to experience. Time is passing by as you are still staring at that phenomenal blank page. The stress starts to conquer a field in your mind. A shadow called depression is coming closer and closer, and your heart beat is speeding while you start to accept that state, which until now could only happen to other average writers.

W. Somerset Maugham once said something wise "There are three rules for writing a novel. Unfortunately, no one knows what they are". I am sure he already tasted at that moment what you are only now tasting... the writer's block. And yes, maybe those three rules were not yet discovered but for sure in ancient times, the people called Feng Shui practitioners announced and proved remedies for so many situations such as this. Did they know at that moment that you will be in this predicament? Who can answer this question? Maybe yes, maybe no... who knows how the informational energy flows in time and space?

But for sure they developed techniques that can help you overcome this phase.

1. One of the most powerful helpers is adding gently moving clear water and placing it near you.

- As the water flows, in exactly the same way your words will soon start to flow again.

- As the water drips, in the same way your creativity will begin to drip.

- As the water glides, the productivity you need will again start to glide.

2. Add an additional flower or plant on your desk and this will expand your writing skills again.

3. Place quotes of writers whom you admire on your desk.

- They will release the stress that conquered you.

4. Avoid distractions by un-cluttering your mind.

- Yes, you heard well: un-clutter your mind of all those hundreds of simultaneous thoughts that you are having.

- Relax and don't think that you must check your Twitter and Facebook accounts, or read your emails and all those newsletters with advice for writers.

- Simply relax your mind and let the words come back to you.

5. Choose what is best for your personality: either go take a walk with nature or close the door of your office and meditate in solitude.

- Whatever is suitable for you, it will help to center yourself again, and the creativity will revisit you once more.

6.2 - THE WRITER'S ZONE

To understand what a writer's zone is, you must first experience the previous state called a writer's block. Then and only then will you understand how you can face it and how you can move to the writer's zone. This zone is exactly the opposite of a writer's block; it is the optimal phase in which a writer can find himself. It is the phase in which Chi flows freely on the writer's path, the creativity is boosted and the writing productivity reaches maximum level.

Having knowledge about both states, a writer's block and a writer's zone, you can save the wasted time between these two phases.

There are some elements that influence your entering into this zone.

- One of these is your location. Depending on where you live, you must find a writing environment that boosts your writing mood. Find a place suitable for you that you feel relaxed in and totally prepared to let the words flow.

- Take a walk in the park or the woods, go for a drive on a long unpopulated road. Don't forget to take the camera with you and take pictures that will help you relax the next time you need to enter into the writer's zone without having to walk again. A walk in a quiet and relaxing place is a good Feng Shui method to un-clutter your mind of stress.

- Do some brainstorming for your future book; try to prepare a good plot for your novel. Do some research on the theme that you want to write about.

- Avoid emails, other online temptations, phones and any other distractions that are blocking the Chi flow of your creativity and productivity.

- Listen to some music and prepare a playlist with your favorite relaxing songs. Use this list until it becomes a habit that is helping you enter into the writer's zone.

- Breathe! Yes, breathe. Fill your lungs with fresh air until they expand to the point where they touch, take a small pause then exhale slowly. Learn to breathe again, so the good Chi also enters your body.

- Burn some incense and use aromatic lamps for fragrance.

- Find a writing retreat in your area. Make it a part of your writing process. This will always get you into the zone. There are two kinds of retreats: solo retreats (suitable for writers who prefer solitude far away from any distractions including other writers) and group retreats (provides a chance for face to face group brainstorming). The best writing retreats are those that include both solo and group retreats. When you go to a writing retreat, be sure that you are applying the Feng Shui principles in that place also (you can even take a Bagua map with you).

- If your mind feels unclear in ideas, use a yellow vase where you place orange flowers. This will boost the intensity of your writing and will give you the necessary clarity.

- Don't forget to always include the water element in your space.

- Avoid too many electronic devices in the moments when you write because they will drain your energy, and soon you'll have to face another writer's block.

- Hang a wooden chime near you so its movement will activate any stagnant Chi.

6.3 - THE CREATIVE MIND

To talk about Creativity and to try to tell all that can be told, we will probably need a lifetime. And after this we would want to come back in human bodies, to reincarnate for the same reason that we still have something more to tell about it.

To keep this short because our book is about Feng Shui the writer's creativity and not about the creative mind itself, we will mention that creativity is a phenomenon through which something worthwhile and original is created. The final product can come in various forms, and this depends on the subject or area of interest. Creativity is not a science or knowledge but a skill that can be improved through different methods.

There are several theories on creativity, and all are investigating the reasons for which some people are more creative than others. There can be multiple reasons for this, but the main factors were identified and named as "the four Ps". They are the process, the product, the person and the place.

1. To focus on the creative process, it means to focus on mechanisms and techniques for creative thinking.

2. To focus on the creative product, it means to measure creative ideas according with their success.

3. The focus on the nature of the creative person, it means to analyze the intellectual habits (openness, autonomy, expertise, behaviors, etc.)

4. And finally to focus on the place, it means to pay attention to circumstances in which the creativity is boosted and flourishes.

And here comes our art… Feng Shui.

For sure, you can't give someone a shot of creativity like you are doing when injecting a medicine into their veins. But you can create the environmental conditions to get the best out of them.

To be creative, it means to trust in you. It means instead of asking yourself why something has happened when you see it happening, as others are asking, instead see what it could be and ask yourself "Why not?"

A creative mind observes information through the world around, finds the relationship between the facts and just connects the dots, creates new original and useful products. And what can be more useful than a book created by the writer?

Ultimately, creativity is the result of how you think; to open your mind and to create the best environmental conditions for your writing process also belongs to the way you think. This is called creative thinking, and it allows you to break all the barriers.

Some of these barriers are there in front of your eyes, but you can't see them because they have energetical roots. But you can receive the keys called Feng Shui techniques, and with them open the locks that temporarily keep the gates to creativity closed.

Those closed gates are, in fact, the stress that makes us loose time being trapped in a mental blockage. The ability to reduce this amount of stress can be boosted by Chi flow; use this ancient art, and you will attract fresh creative energy necessary for your writings.

So, how can we create the best Feng Shui environment to support and boost your creativity? To Feng Shui a creative process called writing, performed by the creative person named a Writer, it always implies making space for something that is still not perceived but has a potential of manifestation through energetic approaches.

To Feng Shui a space doesn't mean that you have to create a peaceful place in which you have to meditate. To the contrary, it means to create a space in which the energy will give you all that you need to connect the creative dots so your final product will see the Light. And more than this, it can also be seen by others.

So, don't expect to Feng Shui your space to meditate if you are writing a historical book about wars, or if you approach the fantasy novels where demons and monsters are surrounding your main character. It's obvious that for this, you need to boost the fire element in your environment. And the examples can continue but I am sure you already caught the main idea. This book is about this; each chapter is trying to particularize the Chi flow for optimal conditions for all categories of Writers.

Being a writer myself, I recently started to work on my first novel. This book is intended to be a mix of romances, fantasy, paranormal, spiritual and probably some more genres. While preparing the plot for the book, I decided to include hidden meanings between the lines, so all type of readers would find more than just words and facts inside. The book will be written with a personal technique (yes, I am very creative). Depending on the level the reader has reached on the spiritual ladder, the written words will uplift and bring to surface knowledge already known; this knowledge was blocked or forgotten when the choice was made to come on this planet and into these human bodies.

To make the explanation short, while I was working on the novel, I realized that my surroundings didn't influence me as I wanted.

I suddenly noticed that the Chi flow around my desk and office was stagnant for what I needed to write. Instantly the cogwheels in my brain started working at a high-speed level, and a new creative idea was born... I have to Feng Shui my office, to let the Chi flow freely, to accurately boost my environment for this writing project. I did it... and for some time I wrote like never before; I almost couldn't be stopped by any external influences.

But... after a while I realized something; I couldn't keep this information only to myself. I had to share it with my fellow writers. Thus started the process I dubbed "the birth of my second first book". Yes, like this I referred to my project through which the book "Feng Shui for Writers" was born. I called it "the birth" because even the smallest ideas we have, cross through a birth process before manifesting into this world. I called it "my second first book" because it is my first published book, but the second one to be implemented and emerge from the embryo phase.

And this book was born **for YOU - the Writer**!

A flash of light… a flash of creativity… I just realized that what I just wrote, it best explains the reasons for writing this book and what it is about. Well… what I've said up to now has only been a simple flash of light. The flesh of creativity is the fact that I will include this passage at the beginning of this book, practically quoting myself.

Sounds weird doesn't it? Like all newly created things look in their moments of birth. But we are now talking about creativity, and what better example could we give than to do something that maybe no one has done until now… quoting from your own words in the same book!

Or maybe someone has done it before without my knowledge. In this case, we can enter into another zone of interest which talks about the collective souls, about accessing information that you had no idea you can access… and so on… But believe me… even if the subject is somehow related to our present domain of interest, we will not dig any further inside it now. I love to take things step by step. But if you, the reader want… another book can be born. "Ask, and it shall be given to you," said a very wise predecessor.

All you have to do is really wish, and after this to ask. Exactly as in our case; you want to write, you wish to access and to completely bring to surface your hidden creativity. All you have to do now is to ask for it, and the solution will be given to you; in fact, several methods from which to choose from.

I invite you to choose the ancient art of Feng Shui and its deep techniques.

To focus on attracting the best Feng Shui energy into your creative zone, you should first answer to some questions that will help you make the best decision, so your dream, desire, and plan will find the optimum manifestation in time and space:

1. What is my exact activity and to what writing genre does it belong to?

2. What are the feelings and the states of mind which I must have while I am writing, so my final book will be exactly as I want it to be?

3. What additional activities should I perform, in order to well prepare the start of my project?

4. What state of mind should I experience while performing the additional activities?

5. Which Feng Shui remedies should I choose for each crossing phase of my project?

6. Can I find a common remedy (except un-cluttering my internal and external world) so all my actions will be covered by it, or should I separate the moments in time and space by applying several remedies?

7. What path do I choose to finalize my writing project knowing that the Beginning and the End of any Creation has the same Root... My First Thought?

After you decide what your final answers to these questions will be, read this book again. You will understand and will bring to the surface much more than you did reading it the first time.

To conclude, even if we could probably talk a lot more about the writer's creativity, to Feng Shui the writer's space evokes the same energy that belongs to the writer's brilliant creative process.

Feng Shui is not Magic. Feng Shui is an Art, a Technique and an Ancient science describing how to work with energies while we are here in these human bodies. We use it to control the Chi flow in order to obtain what we want in life, and accomplish our reason for being here.

6.4 - STRESS RELIEVERS

To find remedies for any perturbation, we must first understand what that perturbation is and what its roots are.

For a human being, any perturbation in their peaceful theoretical life which he should have is called Stress. This is an emotional or mental state caused by unfavorable or demanding circumstances.

Usually, we say that we are stressed when we are overloaded, and we are unsure if we can or cannot cope with that pressure. While in stressful situations, there are several effects on our bodies that we can feel: the blood pressure and pulse rise, the digestive system slows down, breathing is accelerated, muscles become tense and sleep is probably not as good as before.

We will not analyze stress too much; the purpose of our book is to bring remedies, and anyway, we all know at some level or another, what stress is and how it makes you feel.

With our field of interest being Feng Shui, let's see how we can incorporate stress relievers into our lives. For writers, there are several points that we should mention:

1. Choosing furniture with round corners will reduce the Shar Chi pointed to us, and this will keep irritability to a minimum level.

2. Positioning any sharp corners of furniture or decorative objects out of traffic's way will maintain the immune system (including the emotional immune system) at maximum level.

3. Avoiding hard lighting, sparkling and glaring light, will reduce irritability, exhaustion, and petulance.

4. Adding music (each writer's category will probably need different types of music, according with the main theme of their projects) will help you reach the state of mind which you need at that moment. It is better to listen to only instrumental music so the potential lyrics will not disturb the flow of your thoughts while you are writing.

5. Running water will maintain a high level of satisfaction.

6. Incense and essential oils will help in raising your mood, reducing anxiety and aiding focus and concentration. The most popular incense fragrances for stress relief are lavender, cypress and rosemary. You must be careful to use the exact incense your body needs; each person being sensitive to different fragrances. I am sure you don't want to use incense that will make you feel sick, even if your writer friend told you that for him that essence is like a treasure.

7. Placing a crystal near you will assure all the conditions that any poison arrow or negative energy thrown your way will be absorbed instantly. You'll find a special chapter in this book about this subject.

8. In the periods when money and clients seemed to disappear, the writer can cross that special phase named the "writer's block". We already talked about remedies for this case, so maybe you will want to go back to read through that chapter again.

9. Don't forget to clean and organize your desk and office; this will protect you from many possibly stressful phases.

10. Maybe it sounds like a joke but one of the best stress relievers that we can use while we are writing, is to close the door of our office to add a separation fence between us and the rest of the world; anyway we need to be in another world… our book's world, our article's world, our whatever world we need to be in when we write.

11. Keep away from your phone, radio, TV, or any source of information which can influence the flux of your own thoughts while you are writing. These are powerful sources of stress for a writer who needs to immerse in his creativity.

12. And the last one but not the least is to sleep. Sleep enough for your body to release any shadow of stress. Our bodies have a phenomenal capacity to relieve any perturbation and to cure themselves. Use the Feng Shui art for this; no, we will not talk about this because it is a subject for another book.

I am not saying that by doing all this in your life there will never appear a stressful situation. I am saying that if you apply the Feng Shui techniques and remedies whenever you will encounter a situation like this, your power to overcome will be boosted and after a short time, you will not even remember what hit you (no, don't think you will lose your memories; no way! You will only understand that it is nothing there to remember to stress you even more). And here's some more on this... after a while you will look at a stressful situation like something funny and necessary. And that is because you will suddenly have the power to see behind the appearances, and you will know that life would be very boring without any stress. This is somehow a joke, but you know that any joke contain a seed of truth.

So, let's accept the source of stress, let's use Feng Shui remedies to cure the effects and let's go on after this. Life is so beautiful in fact, and we have much more books to write, to fill the reader's heart with contentment and happiness.

7
CRYSTALS FOR WRITERS

Magnifying creativity is a desire that any writer should have. This creativity can also be influenced by using the power of crystals.

When the changes will be noticed, you can also observe that not only the creativity was enhanced but many aspects of your life have also improved. You can also reveal many things that were buried inside you that you had no idea about.

As a writer, you have multiple choices in making this change. There are particular crystals that develop your potential and which can unlock what was hidden until now. New skills will suddenly come to the surface, and you will be able to control and take your life in a new direction.

The crystals work on higher spiritual levels and together with developing your creativity, will also have an effect on your health state.

If you use them on a regular basis, the change will be rapidly noticed due to their influence over your aura, which brings to you positive vibrations and change for the better.

If you want to make a study on the crystal's effect on your life, you can keep a daily journal of your observations; anyway, you are a writer, aren't you?

The Feng Shui crystals disperse the yang energy that is brought into the office by sunlight. Decorating your windows with crystals is a very good and interesting method, which can improve the quality of the light that enters the room. The rainbow that will be created by these crystals will make you feel pleasant and comfortable.

You can also place them in a bowl on your desk or anywhere you need inspiration and imagination.

Do you need special training or skills to use crystals? Of course you don't need any special training. The crystals work even if you don't have deep knowledge about them.

However, it is good to remember to cleanse your crystals once a month; this is because they are taking the lower energies from you. Some people recommend cleaning them with water and salt, but usually it's enough just to put the crystal under the sun for a whole day.

A crystal has many degrees of functions, but we will only list here the effects that can be beneficial to the writer. Even if the reason for needing a crystal is to overcome a writer's block, to unleash the imagination and increase the creativity a writer can change the evolution of the personal writing process using its help.

Example of crystals that can be of great influence for a writer:

- **Citrine** opens the mind and brings new thoughts. Citrine really boosts your confidence (useful when you've received rejection letters, and you think you are not as good as you expected to be).

- **Garnet** encourages the imagination and makes you take action when it is needed.

- **Ametrine** brings intuition for success by combining the qualities of amethyst and citrine.

- **Sodalite pyramids** - if the writers keep a sodalite sphere or pyramid on their writing desk it helps with overcoming writer's block.

- **Chalcedony** is also called the stone of orators; enhances the ability to communicate and translate ideas into action. Opens inspiration.

- **Dioptase** increases the imagination and creativity.

- **Amber** encourages creativity and boosts self-confidence.

- **Rhodochrosite Sphere** boosts the creative process and the playfulness mood.

- **Jade** stimulates ideas and spontaneity.

- **Carnelian** increases the creative energy and also helps release stress. It has a very warming energy and is good for those who encountered a writer's block.

- **Iolite** unlocks the writer's creativity.

- **Ruby** increases passion as a driving force.

- **Golden Labradorite** is a crystal that also boosts creativity.

- **Blue topaz stone** is called the writer's stone. It increases the ability to communicate better and to express meaningfully both speaking and writing.

- **Prehnite crystals** help focus and enhance your wisdom, lighting your path to understanding.

- **Tiger's Eye** breaks those creative blocks and gets the

words running freely again. It also encourages contact with other people, so it is very useful for the writer who has a tendency to isolate themselves.

- **Kyanite** is a blue stone that governs communication in all forms whether spoken or written.

As a general rule, keep orange crystals around you to boost your creative mind, blue crystals to help your communication, and clear crystals such as Quartz to help your clarity of thought.

8

COLOR YOUR WORLD

One of the best methods to Feng Shui your working place is to use colors. You can easily transform any office into an elevating and stimulating environment if you study and understand the color psychology.

Colors have a silent language that has its own vibration exactly like music has. If you know how to use them, you can manipulate the viewer's perception but you can also manipulate the flow of energy.

Experiencing colors is at the same time an objective and a subjective action.

It is objective because as the studies say, there is a collective unconscious reaction to colors, and this reaction was inherited from our ancestors. This is one aspect that belongs to what is called "the color psychology."

Another aspect that must be mentioned here is the conscious symbolism of colors. Due to this symbolism, the colors have a huge psychological and physical influence on you. At the moment when you understand this effect, you can start to use them in order to create a specific reaction; this reaction can be created in a person or the flow of energies.

Colors influence your brainwaves, your hormonal activity, and your nervous system. Try to sit in a totally red room and after that, check your blood pressure; then move into a completely blue room and notice how you feel.

All of these mentioned above proves the statement that the experiencing of color can be objective.

But at the same time, as we already mentioned, it can be subjective. This subjectivism is caused by personal preferences and reactions to colors.

To make changes in your writing environment so as to determine the needs for Chi to be balanced, you can play with these colors.

Bellow, we will mention the general and objective meanings of colors, and in this way you will have all the details to Feng Shui your desk or room where your office is.

1 - Red is a dynamic color that is activating, stimulating and exciting your senses and at the same time it gives you feelings of power and passion. So...

- If you are a novelist writer, a screenwriter or a playwright that must create fighting scenes or very passionate romantic moments, add on or near your desk some red to inspire you.

- If you are a speechwriter and you want to instill passion in your audience, while you prepare your future speech make sure that your eyes will rest on something red.

- If you are a critic and want to focus on the negative aspects of the object of your interest, add some red Feng Shui objects on your desk. However, at the same time, try to mix the view with a color that will keep a balance inside your critic instincts. Otherwise, you will succeed to ruin someone's career, and for sure no one writes so bad as to deserve such a treatment from you.

2 - Orange is a color that gives you a cheerful and sociable attitude, and at the same time activates and stimulates your senses.

- It is not as arousing as the red color, and its stimulation is very pleasant.

- It is a color that should keep the attention of novelists, poets, lyricists, librettists, biographers, editors, bloggers, journalists, columnists, and memoirists.

- Generally speaking, this should color the writing life of any writer who must maintain a passionate attitude but which must not be too sharp.

3 - Yellow is a bright color that can make you restless and at the same time can instill in your heart a feeling of happiness and warmth.

- It makes people more communicative.

- Yellow encourages optimism and hope.

- The intellect is stimulated and the attention becomes focused through this color.

- So, if your writings are based on humor, you should definitely have yellow Feng Shui items on your desk.

- If you are a satirist, a speechwriter, researcher, letter writer, scribe or report writer use this color on your desk; your work will easily flow, and your communication's power will increase.

4 - Green is a very tranquil, relaxing, balancing, and healing color.

- It stimulates vitality, abundance and is very inspiring.

- Green balances both mind and body.

- No matter what kind of writer you are and which genre you prefer, make sure that on your desk and in your office there is plenty of green.

- If by chance you have to focus for a long time on writing due to a deadline that you must respect, add the color green to your office and this will boost your resistance.

5 - Blue is a color that calms, relaxes and heals.

- It is increasing the contemplation state, the creativity and the desire for spirituality.

- Add lots of blue in your office if you are a poet, biographer, encyclopedist, essayist, translator, memoirist or writer of sacred texts.

- Of course, it is great to have blue near you no matter what you write, but the mentioned categories need more than the rest.

6 - Purple is a color that represents nobility, dignity, abundance, intuition and spirituality.

- All categories of writers should add some purple on their desk.

7 - White can be sterile and detached.

- A white desk energizes the mind but drains the body.

- White increases the desire for spirituality, purity, hopes and helps you have an opened mind.

8 - Black is an introspected and mysterious color.

- It gives power and elegance.

- Black encourages introspection and moves energy down and in.

- No matter what type of writer you're included in, if you feel that black is for you, then go for it!

- Power, mystery, elegance... who doesn't need it when writing a book?

9 - Brown is grounding you and gives you a motherly feeling.

- It is a stable color, and it will influence your writing, making it reliable.

- Having brown furniture in your office, your body will be comforted.

- Brown color is most suitable for writers from the following categories: children's books writers, speechwriters, biographers, critics, editors, encyclopedists, lexicographers, historians, researchers, translators, diarists, journalists, columnists, memoirists, technical writers, and report writers.

- The novelists and poets who write fantasy books would be advised to avoid brown around their desk.

- If, for some reasons, this can't be avoided, then it is necessary to balance the earth element with the other four about which we already talked about.

10 - Gray is a neutral color that lacks energy.

- It is calm and quiet and for sure your physical body will not feel energized having gray around it.

- Still, the brain will focus very well on a specific theme, even if the body will be drained.

- For this reason, you should have gray on your desk or on your office walls if you are a report writer, a technical writer, letter writer, translator, journalist, researcher, historian, encyclopedist, critic, etc.

11 - Silver is a color that reduces anxiety and creates peace.

- It has a strong connection with water and metal and increases clarity, mental power, vision, and intellect.

- All types of writers should design their office by including this color.

12 - Gold is a sophisticated color that evokes luxury, wealth, and splendor.

- If you are a historian, a novelist whose chosen theme is the millionaires' lives or a writer of sacred texts, use the gold color as much as possible; you will receive plenty of inspiration.

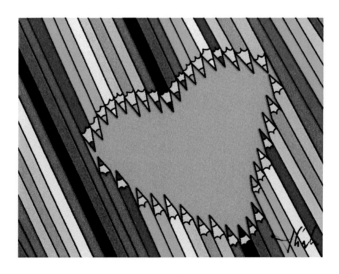

Generally speaking, the influence of colors in our office, our writing mood and capacity is as we mentioned above. What we didn't mention, and it's a must when we are working with energies, is that we always have to listen to our hearts. The subconscious mind already has all the information inside it. If we learn how to listen to our hearts, and trust what it's telling us, then we will always make the right decision for our needs.

So if, for example, we feel the need to have around us a specific color in the office, I advise you to do whatever is necessary for you to have it. Even if the manuals are telling you a different thing. Especially when we are talking about the influence of colors, we need to understand that this is somehow subjective because they also have cultural references and a biological influence. For this reason, when we decide to use a color, we have to examine it with our hearts, the depth of their roots in our transcendent cultural history.

9

PLANTS FOR THE OFFICE

Using the power of plants, we can purify the air and raise the energy in a writer's room.

If the quality of the indoor air is improved so will our writing process.

Can we use the ancient technique of Feng Shui art to do this? Yes, of course we can.

The ideal Feng Shui key is to decorate our office with plants that purify the air.

Here are some examples of plants that will do their best to clear the air and fill it with oxygen:

1. Areca Palm

- Scientific Name: Chrysalidocarpus Lutescens
- Removes all tested indoor air toxins.
- Areca Palm is very easy to care for and a very popular plant.
- Its leaves flow will soften the energy in the office.

2. Rubber Plant

- Scientific Name: Ficus Robusta
- It removes most pollutants and toxins from any room.
- This plant tolerates low temperatures and doesn't need too much light to survive.

3. Bamboo Palm

- Scientific Name: Chamaedorea Seifrizii
- Removes toxins from the air.
- It adds a peaceful feeling to the office and is very resistant to insect infestation.

4. Lady Palm

- Scientific Name: Rhapis Excelsa
- Removes indoor pollutants.
- It is one of the best plants used to improve the indoor air quality.

- It is also very popular and easy to care for.

5. English Ivy

- Scientific Name: Hedera Helix
- Removes pollutants from indoor air.
- It is an easy to grow plant and is very adaptable except at very high temperatures.

6. Dracaena Janet Craig

- Scientific Name: Dracaena Deremensis Janet Craig
- Removes most pollutants and chemical toxins.
- It is an attractive plant that doesn't need much light to grow.

7. Dwarf Date Palm

- Scientific Name: Phoenix Roebelenii
- Removes air pollutants.
- It can tolerate low levels of light.

8. Boston Fern

- Scientific Name: Nephrolepis Exaltata "Bostoniensis"
- Removes most pollutants.
- It has a beautiful aspect and doesn't need any special attention.

9. Ficus Alii

- Scientific Name: Ficus Macleilandii "Alii"
- Removes air toxins.

- It is easy to care for.

- If you move it to a new place, don't be worried if it will lose some leaves. It will recover quickly.

10. Peace Lily

- Scientific Name: Spathiphyllum sp.

- Removes pollutants from indoor air.

- It is an easy to care for plant.

- It gives a peaceful, strong energy.

10
LIGHT FOR WRITERS

Together with all other aspects that can be Feng Shui improved we must take care of the lighting aspect.

Feng Shui is about energy, and we already know that light is the strongest manifestation of this energy. The way in which we light our offices, no matter whether we are talking about natural or artificial light, influences the quality of our work also.

Even if this chapter is placed in the final part of the book, the lighting theme should be the first to always be taken into consideration when we want to positively Feng Shui our working place. The quality and quantity of light must be seriously taken into consideration because this is influencing our health, wellbeing, the power of communication and the creativity essential for a writer.

The light can be natural or artificial, and we will separately talk about it.

When it is about our indoor office, natural light can influence the quality of our work in cases where it is too strong. If the windows of our office are facing the west, the light can sometimes create visual and physical discomfort. If it is too bright and hot, we can adjust its influence using blinds and curtains that can protect us from excessive light and heat.

To Feng Shui the outside light that enters into our office space, the best solution is to use blue color curtains. The blue represents the water element and creates a cool effect over the environment, increasing our productivity.

For the same effect, we can also use blinds and curtains of white color which symbolize the metal element.

There are many voices that have already started to state that light is the first element that we need to feed our bodies with, and for this reason they call it the medicine of the future. So paying attention to the quality of the external or indoor light that has an influence on our working place should become a permanent habit for us.

We talked above about the times when light is too strong but similarly we need to mention the situation in which the sunlight is deficient, and we need to replace it with an artificial source. Of course, in this case, we need to use indoor lights, and here we must mention the fact that from all the sources, fluorescent lighting is the most harmful to human behavior, abilities, and health.

There are lots of studies about fluorescent light and its negative influence. There are countries that have even banned the use of the cool white fluorescent lights. It is not our interest to enter into too many details about this subject now but all we need is to keep in mind that if we as writers want to Feng Shui our office, we need to be aware of that aspect. So, of course if we can, it is largely preferable to open our windows and let the sunlight in.

As with any place, in our offices there can also be what we call problem areas. These are spaces that due to the building's configuration, we can't make an evident change; in these cases we can calm down or even stop the negative influence of this configuration using different methods and one of them is using a good light.

We talked at the beginning of this book about Chi. It is very important to balance it in our working space. A home that is too dark will have too much yin energy. This can be fixed using windows. In case that the surface of the window can't assure sufficient natural light to coming in, we can remedy this by studying the lighting placement within our rooms.

Lamps are the best and an easy way to introduce more light in certain areas of our offices. Because a writer's office is used predominantly for reading and writing, it is necessary for the light we introduce to adequately produce a comfortable feeling when these activities are performed.

To balance the chi and to introduce more yang energy, we can use both floor lamps and table lamps.

The floor lamps brighten up dark corners, and we also have to admit that having a Torchiere lamp inside the office is a very interesting decorative element. The light from these types of lamps shine up towards the ceiling and reflect back onto the working space.

The wall lighting also has a very positive influence on the chi; sometimes this kind of lighting can be more expensive due to structural problems, so you may wish to use the floor lamps instead.

It is important to mention, that if we prefer a ceiling light, we must avoid a low suspended light fixture that hangs from the ceiling. In Feng Shui, this kind of light hanging is considered to be very inauspicious for all the people who enter into that room. For a writer, the office is the main room that's used daily, so we will never want to be influenced by this manifested energy.

Another inauspicious situation is one caused by multi-faceted lights that cast shadows on the ceiling or walls. The explanation is that in a writer's office the yang energy given by the light must be predominant and not the yin energy caused by the dark shadows.

One very important aspect when we talk about Feng Shui is the light influence in the entrance zone of our office. If the outside door is properly illuminated, this attracts positive chi inside. For this reason, make sure that whenever the outside light bulb is burned out, immediately replace it with a functional one. For writers, this means to attract a continuous flow of creativity inside the working place.

We already know that light symbolizes the fire energy. For this reason, we can also use the light to balance the problems caused by a house that has a predominant wood energy. Whenever we illuminate an area, we are activating the Yang Chi in that space.

To create an auspicious and good fortune working place we have to:

1. Identify the sectors which need to be energized.

If we read up to this point, we already know what a Bagua map is. This eight sided symbol represents the eight directions that are influencing the flow of energy.

- The North represents career luck, so if you want to have a long and prolific writing career, you have to illuminate this direction properly.

- The South brings fame and recognition, and these are very important for the writer's career.

- The East brings good health and like in any other profession, for the writer to be creative and relaxed, good health is very important.

- The West brings descendants luck.

- The North-East is for education, so especially if you are an editor, a researcher, or an academic writer you have to take care of this direction in a special way.

- The North-West is for making friends and mentor luck. Light up this direction also because you don't want to be a lonely writer without any connection. To be published and to make yourself known you need good connections.

- The South-East represents wealth and riches. In case that you make a living from your writing activity, you need to take care of this direction also.

- The South-West is for love. In case that your novels talk about romance, this direction is a very easy way to handle your romantic creativity. And it is not only about creativity here. By maintaining a good flow of energy in this direction, you can also meet the love of your life and not through your writings only. And when you attract your soul mate to you, all your abilities will suddenly increase, and together with them your creativity also. You will practically receive wings, so take good care of the South-West direction.

2. Work with light through colors.

We already talked about the power of colors when we Feng Shui our office. This power can be used when it is combined with light also. The mixed power is even stronger than using them separately.

First we identified the sectors of our writing place that we want to enhance. To Feng Shui those using the colored light we need to know that:

- The colorless or white light is the most conservative because the white color embodies the whole spectrum of colors. Using it is a very welcomed decision.

- If we want to be more imaginative in using and decorating our working place with colors, we need to pick a color that harmonizes with the preponderant energies from a specific sector.

- As we already know, the energies are characterized by the five elements: fire, earth, metal, water and wood.

- The correspondences between colors of light and the elements are:

    o   Fire is red, and South is associated with this color.

    o   Earth is yellow and is associated with South-West, North-East, and the Center.

    o   Metal is white and is associated with West and North-West directions.

    o   Water is blue and is associated with North.

    o   Wood is green and is associated with East and South-East.

- When you Feng Shui your office with colored lights, you need to make sure to use the white light which contains all the elements, or use a color associated with the element of the sector which you need to illuminate.

3. Play with symbols and statues.

- Combined with proper lighting, the symbols and statues will give more energy, bringing you the power to attract positivity into your writing life.

- The most auspicious esoteric objects are dragon-tortoises, three legged toads, and the more ordinary Chi statues such as horses, elephants, birds, and crystals.

- To Feng Shui your writing place, you have to avoid sharp pointed sculptures and scary looking decorative patterns. You should always feel comfortable looking at the used symbols and statues.

- Feel free to use your imagination when it is to combine lighting with these symbols. The light is filling the esoteric symbol with additional energy and will create auspicious conditions for the natural flow of your creativity.

4. Decide what kind of light you need: strong light or soft light.

- A direct light or a fluorescent one is considered strong lighting.

- An indirect light or a yellow one is considered soft lighting.

- Strong lighting is better suited in the office areas. If somehow your writing place is common with the bedroom area, avoid hard light as much as possible.

- If you want to activate only a corner of the office, then use soft lighting by choosing a lampshade or lava lamp.

5. Avoid illuminating certain sectors.

- We call them taboo sectors, and they should not be illuminated too much.

- These areas include bathrooms, storerooms and kitchens that are near our writing office.

- At the moment when you are not using these spaces, keep their doors closed and try not to make them more prominent than the working place that is much more important to highlight.

11
TIPS FOR ATTRACTING PRODUCTIVITY, SUCCESSFUL PUBLISHING, AND MONEY

Being a writer you need to not only concentrate on increasing your creativity, but also on productivity, success and money.

There is no reason for you to be creative only from time to time and not use this creativity on a long term basis which will in turn attract the needed success, and of course a good financial situation. No writer needs to be a hero who writes only for others yet starves doing it.

So, the Feng Shui of your writing office determines your success, your reputation, the needed productivity and the reflected financial bonuses. An office which has a good Feng Shui is noticed by your guests also and by your writing partners such as editors, publishers, agents, and so on, who need to pay visits to your place due to the permanent collaboration between you and them.

From this point of view, your office should give them a warm and a welcoming sensation. When this energy is felt, both you and your partners feel more confident and optimistic when you interact. The inner balance of your office is transferred to the relation between you and your visitors. So, in these conditions you will collaborate with them to experience a peak performance level.

To see your career flourish, apply all that you've learned until now in this book. Evaluate the place, make the necessary adjustments and notice how they are reflected in the relation between you and your partners, even if they are long-term collaborators or only temporary ones. Observe the results in the high-level productivity and better outputs.

The following tips will help you becoming more productive even if you work at a home office or in an office environment.

1 - Evaluate your working hours, set the program and keep it even if you don't have a boss when working at home.

- You can consider this tip as Feng Shui your time.

- This schedule will give energy signals to your brain that it's writing time, and all your internal system will collaborate to make you write inspired pieces.

2 - When you are writing, set your mind to stay off online temptations.

- If you can't resist it, then make a supreme decision and unplug any device that can connect to the internet.

- Keep working on only the writing devices, and do your job.

- If it is necessary for you to check any websites at specific hours of the day (for example banking or something similar), then set this action in your schedule and don't allocate more than 15 minutes to do this.

3 - Also, fix the hourly period when you will check your emails and do it only during that scheduled time.

- Reply only to urgent emails and the rest of them postpone until you finish your writing scheduled time.

4 - Take frequent breaks after working in stints of 25-30 minutes.

- Refocus your eyes on a distant object and make some body

movements that will help you to relax your muscles.

- During these short breaks stay away from the internet.

- If you don't need such frequent breaks, plan them after 45-50 minutes of writing periods, but make sure you don't skip them.

5 - Separate the writing time from the time allocated to your family.

- Show to everyone in your home that you are serious about this schedule, so everyone will finally respect it.

- Play with your kids only after your daily planned writing time has expired.

- Finally, you are doing this for your family and kids also, to give them a better life through your work.

6 - Don't forget to Feng Shui your writing space so that the Chi will flow properly, and your desk will give you ergonomic comfort.

- Any comfortable sensation that you will have will increase your productivity. And if your productivity is increased as a writer, so too will your success be attracted.

- Unclutter your writing space, free the energy blockage in your writing environment and write your best.

- Take care of your health through Feng Shui because it is practically impossible to be creative and write your best pieces if you are ill.

7 - Also, be aware to keep your desk in the commander position and never sit with your back to the door. This is rule No.1.

- If you can't see what's going on all around you, your work will suffer due to the energy's influence.

- We already talked about this in the above chapters. A writer is a special person who instills his creativity in his characters, ideas and images, to delight the readers.

- So, to do this, the writer has to be sure that the writing environment supports his activity, or else the needed creativity will be dried up.

8 - To increase your productivity and creation add in the South-East corner of your office a small plant or a fountain.

- This will help you grow as a writer.

- Aside from being the corner of creation, the South-East direction is the wealth sector also and if you Feng Shui it, you will attract more incomes based on your writing act.

9 - Use a quartz crystal in the North-East corner of your desk.

- It will help your concentration and your focus on what you need to write.

- This North-East direction is influencing the study act and your wisdom, so placing a crystal there will help you make the best decisions.

10 - If you are trying to establish a contact with a new publisher or you want to market your book properly, then you have to pay special attention to the South wall of your office.

- You already have details from previous chapters about the directions.

- Be sure you position a light to brighten up this wall.

11 - If you want to attract a good payment for your writings, so the prosperity will be positively influenced, target the rear left corner of your desk.

- Put there a plant or a crystal vase.

- The best color to use is purple.

12 - If you want your reputation as a writer and fame to increase, focus on the center back of your desk where the fame space is located.

- You can place there your business cards or a nameplate.
- The color to use is red.

13 - For being productive in writing romances or wanting to have great relationships with your publishers, focus on the rear right corner of your desk.

- Put a fresh flower and a photo with you and your loved one.
- The best color to use for this space is pink.

14 - If you are a reporter or a travel writer, focus on the front right section.

- You can put there a phone or an address book.
- Placing a travel book or photos with the vacation of your dreams is useful in this space.
- The best color to use is gray.

15 - If your goal is to have success in your career, focus on front and center of your desk.

- Pay attention to keeping these places free of clutter.
- The best color, in this case, is black.

16 - If you are an academic or a research writer, pay attention to the front left corner of your desk.

- Place there a proper book for your studying process or a

photo of a genius.

- The best color to use for this place is blue.

17 - If you are a columnist for a health magazine or something similar, focus on the center of your desk and keep it free of clutter to attract a healthy energy.

- The best color to use is yellow.

18 - If you want the absolute best Feng Shui for your writing success and the financial incomes based on your writing, you can place a large fountain in front of your office; of course only if you have the possibility of doing it.

- Pay attention that the water will always be clean and operational.

- Stagnant water will influence your success making it stagnant as well.

- If you want to influence your success and money through a photo, make sure you don't use the destructive type of water images such as huge and crashing waves; this will bring a chaotic creativity and productivity in your career's life.

19 - If you suddenly want to change your writing style and approach a new one, hang a six rod metal wind chime in the career zone of your office.

- Wind chimes are great Feng Shui tools, especially when you want to attract new energies into your writing career.

20 - Decorate your office with images that represent abundance, so creativity, productivity, success, and money will abundantly come into your writing life.

- You can help the flow of energy by using Chinese coins, an abundance ship, a wealth vase, the laughing Buddha, citrine or pyrite crystals.

21 - Use pleasant aromas and scents, candles and fresh flowers in your office.

Music and light are excellent activators of a good energy.

22 - In the money area, avoid a strong Metal and Fire presence, so as to not block the chance of being published and having success with the publishing phase.

12
STUDY AREA FOR CHILDREN'S CREATIVITY BUT NOT ONLY FOR THEM

Well... Yes! Your child is also a writer. As long as he has a desk and homework, you can call him a writer.

I will not dig into this demonstration, but I will add some comments organized in this separate chapter... for your kids only.

Even if your child has a study room or only a writing space in the bedroom, if you Feng Shui this place, you will soon see the results in your kid's life as a student.

Especially in the case in which your child has only a writing space in the bedroom, you have to place the desk and their computer properly.

According with the Feng Shui principles, the best position for your kid's computer desk is closer to the room's entrance door. This stimulates the flowing energy, the yin-yang balance achieved and, as a result, the bedroom will be healthy for your child.

The worst variant is to have a corner desk or a corner computer desk in the bedroom. This will not create good Feng Shui. In case that you already designed your child's bedroom and study space with a desk like this, you can still fix the problems without having to eliminate the desk. Feng Shui is the technique that is giving us solutions to remediate problems energetically using the things that we already own and not to eliminate them. For this, you can improve room layout with Feng Shui solutions like adding greenhouse plants in hanging baskets or pots. These plants will also minimize electrical fields that disturb the Chi.

Additionally, the kids who work at the computer desk should not face the bed. For this, you can use a decorative screen that will hide the bed, or you can replace the bed with a modern sofa. Try to separate the studying and playing areas from beds as much as possible. Place shelves with books near the desk.

In the case of a corner desk, try to leave some space between your desk and the walls. To Feng Shui the room layout it is recommended leaving a 7-9 inch gap. The best position for this kind of a desk is to place it in the corner diagonally opposite to the doorway.

Teach your kid to un-clutter the desk, so the energy will positively influence him.

If you can't afford to place a water fountain in the bedroom, even if the cause is the financial investment or the lack of space, use the color blue to attract same flow as a fountain would. We already know that blue represents water and encourages high thoughts and inner wisdom. If you do this, add some orange accents for contrast and fire.

Also, Feng Shui the writing space included in the bedroom using purple, which represents prosperity and creativity.

Try to use the South wall of the bedroom, placing awards there, diplomas and any detail about the goals your child wants to achieve in the near future.

13
CONCLUSION, CONNECTING THE DOTS

This chapter will be short.

I want you to grasp all of what you read and to find your own conclusion.

Transcribing these in a few words only... I want you to connect the dots.

Don't rush. Don't jump.

It is about your life here.

Relax.

Calm yourself.

Read the book again and...

Your life can be exactly what it is supposed to be... the best time of All your lives.

It is only a matter of TRUST.

I trust you! Do you Trust yourself also?

Listen to your heart!

DO IT YOURSELF... CONNECT THE DOTS!

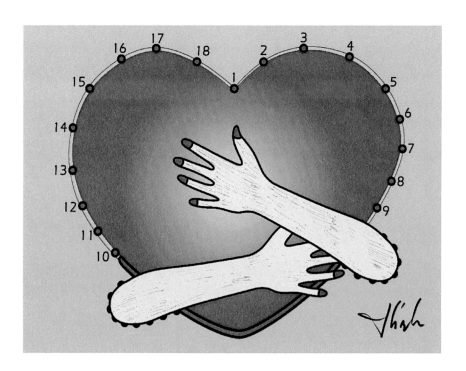

ABOUT THE AUTHOR
MY VERY SHORT BIO

Writer, blogger, translator, researcher, engineer… and much more. What else can I ask for?

I love to study different subjects and different domains. One of my continuous passions is feeling and playing with energies.

I strongly believe that energy is yours free, and you only need to open your heart to regain the lost perception of your true powers. I think that when a student is ready, the teacher appears. For this reason, I've never hunted the information but rather waited for the right moment when I would be ready for the information to find me. Likewise, I know that when someone will need me, the Universe will proceed in such a way that our meeting will take place.

"If you insist to believe that only swimming is possible, you will never learn to fly," says one of my favorite quotes.

Yes, that's me. I believe in the boundless possibilities, which are our birth gifts that we forgot about, and I believe that we are the only ones who are blocking these gifts; blocking them due to our induced beliefs.

I have breathed on this planet since 1967, being born in a country which I always liked, in a city crossed by the Danube river, where my mother was on a short holiday before she was to deliver her first child.

Giving me a musical name, my parents planned out my life since the first days of my existence here. One thing my parents didn't know about was my stubbornness. Instead of using my voice to build my life, I chose to use my technical abilities and became an engineer; a good one in my field of interest. I'm still an engineer as my main activity and for sure I love my job.

In my bio, there's something that needs to be mentioned. I recently decided that I am also a writer. This writer started to ask for her freedom, and I intend to set her free. So, the first move was to choose a Pen Name... like any writer who has a reason to choose one. What's my reason? Only one: intending to write only in the English language, my real name would be hard to spell; but loving too much my name, I simply couldn't get rid of it and decided to only cut out the last few letters.

"Everything is based on contrasts. You can read these lines only because there is enough contrast between the letters and the background".

Yes, that's me also. Fire and ice, sweet and bitter, warm and cold... I will not continue anymore here; I am sure you caught the main idea.

And I am wondering now... can the letters which I will choose bring out enough contrast on the paper to keep your attention awakened?

CONNECT WITH THE AUTHOR

If you want to know more about the author and her writings, you can visit her websites:

- www.MCSimonWrites.com

- www.FengShuiForWriters.com

- www.WritersPayItForward.org

Should you need to contact M.C. Simon directly whether for sharing your stories and life experiences, give feedback or just to say hello, please e-mail her at mcsimon@mcsimonwrites.com - she'd love to hear from you.

FROM THE AUTHOR

If you enjoyed reading the book, found it useful, interesting or even touching... would you please consider leaving a review and recommending it to your friends?

THANK YOU!

28473059R00088

Made in the USA
San Bernardino, CA
07 March 2019